Matthew Sleeth, MD

Blessed Earth

Part 2
Guidebook

P9-DGD-015

Hope for Humanity

 ZONDERVAN®

www.andcross.com

ZONDERVAN.com/
AUTHORTRACKER
follow your favorite authors

ZONDERVAN

Hope for Humanity Guidebook
Copyright © 2010 by Blessed Earth and Dot&Cross

Requests for information should be addressed to:
Zondervan, *Grand Rapids, Michigan 49530*

ISBN 978-0-310-32488-1

All Scripture quotations, unless otherwise indicated, are from the *New Revised Standard Version of the Bible,* copyright © 1989 by the Division of Christian Education of the National Council of Churches of Christ in the United States of America, and are used by permission. All rights reserved.

Scripture quotations marked NIV are taken from the Holy Bible, *New International Version®, NIV®.* Copyright © 1973, 1978, 1984 by Biblica, Inc.™ Used by permission of Zondervan. All rights reserved worldwide.

Scripture quotations marked NASB are taken from the *New American Standard Bible.* Copyright © 1960, 1962, 1963, 1968, 1971, 1972, 1973, 1975, 1977, 1995 by The Lockman Foundation. Used by permission.

Scripture quotations marked NLT are taken from the Holy Bible, *New Living Translation,* copyright © 1996, 2004. Used by permission of Tyndale House Publishers, Inc., Wheaton, Illinois. All rights reserved.

Any Internet addresses (websites, blogs, etc.) and telephone numbers printed in this book are offered as a resource. They are not intended in any way to be or imply an endorsement by Zondervan, nor does Zondervan vouch for the content of these sites and numbers for the life of this book.

All rights reserved. No part of this publication may be reproduced, stored in a retrieval system, or transmitted in any form or by any means—electronic, mechanical, photocopy, recording, or any other—except for brief quotations in printed reviews, without the prior permission of the publisher.

Written by Matthew Sleeth, Nancy Sleeth, and Michael Colletto.
Edited by Michael Colletto.
Produced by Dot&Cross and represented by Kevin Small of smallbooks.com.
Cover and interior design: Seth Herman

Printed in the United States of America

10 11 12 13 14 15 16 /DCI/ 20 19 18 17 16 15 14 13 12 11 10 9 8 7 6 5 4 3 2 1

Dedication

All glory to God.

Contents

How to Use This Guidebook

The *Blessed Earth* film series is designed to challenge God's people to think critically and biblically about the issue of creation care. Whether you are exploring this issue on your own or within a group at home, school, or church, don't feel like you have to read every section or answer every question in this guidebook. Take your time, set your own pace, and simply open your heart to God. Allow Him to use this material to a change your life.

For individuals:

If you have access to your own copy of the DVD and wish to explore the content in greater depth on your own, we recommend that you watch each film session first, then working through the corresponding chapter of this guidebook. If you have time, watch the film a second time to continue to flesh out your answers.

For groups:

If you're sharing a copy of the DVD and exploring the sessions in a group setting, we recommend that you read through each session chapter first in preparation for your group discussion.

Before the session: Read the chapter in advance. This guide was designed to be easy to understand, so you'll be able to answer many of the questions without having seen the films. Answer as many questions as you can (but don't feel like you have to answer them all). Fill out the Action Plan for today, this week, this month, and this year. If you'd rather, simply make a few notes as you read through—whatever helps you feel prepared to meet with your group.

During the session:
1. Watch the film together.
2. If the group is large (more than 10 people), divide into discussion groups of six or fewer. Discuss the session and share your answers and action plans. Do not feel like you must get to every question.
3. If you split up the group, bring everyone back together to share highlights from your discussions and share one or more goals with the whole group.
4. Assign the next chapter.

For group leaders:

You do not need to be a teacher or "expert" to lead a group—you just need a desire to share the call to care for creation. If you're interested in leading a group discussion, please visit blessedearth.org and download the free Leader's Guide for additional ideas and instructions.

Thank you for sharing this journey with us. We are grateful for all you are doing to care for God's creation!

—Matthew and Nancy Sleeth

Introduction

Hope for Humanity is about just that: hope. Our world may be in trouble, but God wants you to help. As members of the "body" of Christ we act as the hands and feet of God's will on the planet. If God loves the world, we should too.

In the first part of this series, we discussed the elements of creation. We examined light, water, soil, heavens, animals and, finally, humans. We saw how these six elements are not only loved by God, but are themselves metaphors of Christ's love for us.

In Part 2, we're going to explore how we live out Christ's love. We'll be focusing not on nouns, but on verbs—on actions.

This isn't about you saving the planet. It's not about you trying really hard to do things right so God won't punish you. It's about your heart. If your heart is overflowing with the love of God, if your heart beats with His, your life—like Christ's—will be different. And your care, compassion, and joyful generosity will breathe hope into a world groaning for redemption.

Ultimately, *Blessed Earth* is about a radical, biblical truth: following Jesus is good for the whole earth—the planet itself and its entire people. In the end, hope for today and hope for tomorrow is found in nothing less than our God at work in us. In His grace and power, may we learn to be better stewards of all He's entrusted into our care.

—Dr. Matthew Sleeth
Executive Director, Blessed Earth

Session 7
Rest

Session Summary

❝ *All who keep the Sabbath without desecrating it and who hold fast to my covenant—these I will bring to my holy mountain and give them joy in my house of prayer.* **❞**

—*Isaiah 56:6–7 (NIV)*

On the seventh day God created rest. He didn't just stop creating things; He created something new, blessed it, and called it holy. And so we begin our series of actions with the indispensable inaction of a day of rest.

Rest doesn't just happen. It's not just the absence of activity. Rest, like all good things, is a gift from God in and of itself. The fourth commandment is really quite simple: stop everything. Relax. *"Remember the Sabbath and keep it holy."* It's the only commandment that begins with "Remember," as if God knew we would forget about it. It's also the longest of the Ten Commandments. God is explicit and all-inclusive: don't work on the Sabbath day—don't make your son or daughter or anyone else in your household work, don't make strangers or illegal aliens or minimum wage employees work, and don't make animals work. Everyone and everything gets a day of rest. We cool our jets. We idle our engines.

Sounds nice, but how do we find rest in a 24/7 world? Just as the Hebrew people were slaves in Egypt, we have become slaves to technology. Cell phones, email, television, and the Internet are our twenty-first century taskmasters. Our technological tools allow 24-hour productivity and connectivity, give us more control … and subtly enslave us to busyness itself.

Sabbath is about restraint, about intentionally *not* doing everything all the time just because we can. Setting aside a day of rest helps us reconnect with our Creator and find the peace of God that passes all understanding. The Sabbath is about letting go of the controls one day a week and letting God be God.

Musicians say that it is not the notes but the pauses between them that make the song. Similarly, the pauses between our workweeks add beauty and meaning to our lives. These Sabbath "stop days" turn the buzz of our busy lives into music.

Reflections on Rest

For years our family kept a weekly day of rest. Then I began preaching in churches around the country almost every Sunday and the trips out of town grew longer and more frequent. There was no longer a rhythm to my life, and I felt the strain—physically, emotionally, and spiritually.

I was regularly speaking about the importance of a day of rest each week and I began to ignore my own advice. In the midst of my self-made whirlwind, God sent me a reminder.

On a rare day home, I opened a letter. It was from a pastor whom I greatly respect. He was writing to encourage me, and to say how much he appreciated my work. At the end of the letter, he added a postscript: "Are you remembering to keep the Sabbath?"

Busted! After enjoying a weekly day of rest for years, somehow in the last few months I had given up my Sabbath.

In case I hadn't gotten the message, I received a second nudge. A few hours after I read the letter, I received a phone call from another pastor. I had spoken at his church some time ago, and he said that my discussion about the Sabbath had really struck a chord—not only for his congregation, but also for him personally. He told me that, for twenty years, he had suffered from depression. But now that he was religiously spending time in nature on his Sabbath, the depression had finally lifted. He was calling just to thank me.

Busted again!

The world gives us clocks; the Lord gives us time. There is more to life than how fast we can get through it. All of us have dozens of commitments, tasks, relationships, and other excuses pulling us away from enjoying the greatest gift of all—rest in God. For a few months, I neglected this gift; I hope that I never do again.

—**Dr. Matthew Sleeth**

Session Notes: Rest

As you watch the seventh session film, **Rest**, feel free to use the following page to jot down any notes, thoughts, and questions.

Hope Begins with a Changed Heart

1 **" *Remember the Sabbath day by keeping it holy.* "**

—*Exodus 20:8 (NIV)*

Do you set aside a weekly day of rest? If not, what stops you? Do you have any traditions on your day of rest, or do you remember any from childhood?

2 **" *Life is about finding and seeking the balance between too much and too little action.* "**

—*Dr. Matthew Sleeth*

Do you maintain a balance of work and rest in your life? If not, what changes can you make to find that balance?

3

> **❝** Sabbath observance invites us to stop. It invites us to rest. It asks us to notice that while we rest the world continues without our help. It invites us to delight in the world's beauty and abundance. **❞**
> —**Wendell Berry, Foreword to Living the Sabbath**

Is working seven days a week a form of pride? How does coming to rest one day a week help us remember that the world doesn't revolve around, or depend on, us?

4

> **❝** Blessed be to God for the day of rest and religious occupation wherein earthly things assume their true size. **❞**
> —**William Wilberforce, British statesman and abolitionist, in his journal about his Sundays**

How does observing a day of rest give God our full attention and help things "assume their true size"?

5 Dr. Sleeth compares the Hebrew people's bondage in Egypt to our bondage to technology and a 24/7 life. "People feel trapped by the technology that was meant to free them. It's not uncommon to hear someone say they cannot give up their technology even if they want to." In what sense has technology become a taskmaster in your life? Give examples.

6 One of the most profound lines in the Bible is, "Be still and know that I am God." How does today's "I'm so busy" mantra distract us from God? Do you make time to "be still" on a regular basis? If not, what changes in your routine would ensure that you make time for God?

Jesus says, "Come to me, all you who are weary and burdened, and I will give you rest. Take my yoke upon you and learn from me, for I am gentle and humble in heart, and you will find rest for your souls. For my yoke is easy and my burden is light." How does this offer from Jesus apply to our 24/7 lives? How is letting go and resting in Jesus a demonstration of faith and trust in his care and provision? What burdens could you place before him today?

8 *" The fourth commandment says we don't make our son or daughter or anyone else in our house work. We don't make strangers or illegal aliens or minimum wage employees work. We don't make anything work—not donkeys or cattle or chickens. We stop. We cool our jets. We idle our engines. "*

—*Dr. Matthew Sleeth*

In addition to taking a day of rest ourselves, we are not supposed to make others work. In what ways do we make others work on the Sabbath? What can we do to encourage others to take a day of rest?

9 *" Stopping is about restraint. It's not about doing everything you can do, but finding the peace of God that passes all understanding. "*

—*Dr. Matthew Sleeth*

In what sense do Sabbath laws (including rest for the land, etc.) encourage restraint?

I'll tell you what my family does on our day of stopping, but remember that you get to decide for yourself. We clean the house the evening before. We don't email. We don't shop. We don't make anyone else work. We nap. We walk outdoors. We rest in rest. If there is an important deadline, we ignore it. We put our trust in God and His promise of rest.

—*Dr. Matthew Sleeth*

Dr. Sleeth describes his day of rest as a "slice of heaven." Describe your ideal day of rest. What would it include? What would it exclude?

11 Dr. Sleeth states, "[T]he Sabbath was not meant to be saved by humanity; humanity was meant to be saved by the Sabbath." Abraham Lincoln stated a similar belief: "As we keep or break the Sabbath day, we nobly save or meanly lose the last and best hope by which man arises."

How can rest "save" humanity? Why does Lincoln call the Sabbath rest our "last and best hope"?

According to Dr. Sleeth, "A day of rest, or restraint, is needed now more than ever." What are some of the outcomes of not taking a day of rest? What would be some of the benefits, both personally and for society, if we took a regular day of rest? Explain the spiritual and environmental impact of working twenty-four hours a day, seven days a week. How can you encourage your church (or school or workplace) to take a weekly day of rest?

12

A Changed Heart = A Changed Life

Of all the steps our family has taken, honoring the Sabbath has given us the most joy. Until the last few decades, America still rested one day a week; a return to this custom could decrease pollution by 10 to 14 percent. Our family avoids driving on Sundays except to go to church, and we don't eat out or make purchases. Instead, we read, talk, listen to music, pray, and go for walks. When we miss a Sabbath day, we feel the negative impact throughout the week. When we honor the Sabbath, we honor our Creator with renewed faith and spirit.

Setting aside a day of rest must be intentional, but there's no real formula. Jesus says that it's the spirit of the law, not the letter, which matters. You may choose to abstain from certain activities on your Sabbath day—no shopping, no Internet, no emailing, no eating out. Or you may choose to spend your Sabbath reading aloud as a family, playing board games, or going on a walk. Once you start observing the Sabbath intentionally, you won't ever want to give it up. The Sabbath way of life can make every day a holy day.

How do you start? Preparing for the Sabbath takes forethought. If you don't want to shop on the Sabbath or you don't want to clean, you need to make sure you've done those things ahead of time. If you don't want work to interfere, you have to wrap things up in advance, let colleagues know that you don't answer calls or email on the Sabbath, and close up shop.

Our family cleans the house the day before the Sabbath; it takes about forty minutes for us to clear up clutter, dust, vacuum, scrub bathrooms, and clean the kitchen. We've been doing this for years. The reward is a relaxed home, with (almost) everything in its place.

Many people begin their Sabbath day with church in fellowship with God's people. However, if you are involved in running the nursery, worship team, choir, worship service, or Sunday school—if, in essence, you "work" at church on Sundays—consider taking an additional day for your day of rest.

Many families, unfortunately, end their Sabbath the moment they leave the church parking lot. Though it might be tempting to stop at the store on the way home from church, avoid running errands on the Sabbath. Our family tries not to engage in any commerce; God wants *all* people to have a chance to rest. It is often minimum-wage earners, today's "menservants and maidservants," who have no choice but to work on weekends.

We need a day when we not only cease working, but also cease worrying about not working. Try putting away anything that reminds you of work. Shut down the computer. Don't answer email. Place your wallet, cell phone, PDA, and unpaid bills in a drawer. Close the door to your home office. Reminders of chores left undone, calls that need to be returned, and long to-do lists will interfere with the rest that God wants us to enjoy.

Consider including an hour of silence in your Sabbath day. To cease is to let God be God and enjoy his presence. One of our favorite Sabbath rituals is to take a Sabbath walk.

Most of all, Sabbath is about resting in God's love. The Sabbath is a time for loving our families and loving our friends. It's about embracing our church families, especially those who are struggling or feeling alone. It's about caring for strangers, inviting them into our homes and our lives. It's about loving God, loving His creation, and loving His living Word, including the commandment to rest. And it's about going into the week ahead, overflowing with Christ's love.

—*Nancy Sleeth*

Adapted with permission from *Go Green, Save Green: A Simple Guide to Saving Time, Money, and God's Green Earth* (Tyndale, 2009)

Good Steward Action Plan: Rest

Instructions

1. Pick two or more new actions from the suggested lists to commit to today, this week, this month, and this year—or come up with your own way to honor the Sabbath.
2. Go to blessedearth.org and join our community of Good Stewards. Plus, you will find additional ideas for becoming a better steward of God's creation.
3. We will send you encouragement throughout the year and help you stay on track with your goals. We're all in this together, so share your journey. Let us know what was easy, what was more difficult, and inspire others with your story!

Today, Lord, help me to:

(pick at least two of the following goals, or come up with your own actions)

- Make a list of things to include and exclude on the Sabbath.
- Talk with my family about when and how we want to celebrate the Sabbath.
- Read Psalm 92.
- Resolve not to run errands.
- Select a family read-aloud book or devotional that I can share.

1. _____

2. _____

This week, Lord help me to:

(pick at least two of the following goals, or come up with your own actions)

- Clean the house before the Sabbath.
- Get all my errands done before the Sabbath.
- Take off my watch and remove all reminders of work on my day of rest.
- Turn off my computer and keep it off all day.
- Use the answering machine to screen calls.
- Encourage my family to rest.
- Observe some quiet time on the Sabbath.
- Read Psalms 23, 24, 29, 93, 126, and 148.

1. _____

2. _____

Adapted with permission from *Go Green, Save Green: A Simple Guide to Saving Time, Money, and God's Green Earth* (Tyndale, 2009)

&& *I was raised in a conservative Jewish home. Every Friday night, we lit the candles, said a blessing over the bread and wine, and shared a Sabbath meal. We frequently added a leaf to the table to make room for family friends. Now, as a Christian family, we incorporate a few of these Hebrew prayers and Sabbath observances. It delights me to remember that Jesus, Mary, and Joseph observed similar traditions in their home.* **""**

—*Nancy Sleeth*

This month, Lord, help me to:

(pick at least two of the following goals, or come up with your own actions)

- Find a church home, if I don't have one already.
- Say grace before meals.
- Take a Sabbath walk.
- Spend at least ten minutes completely surrounded by nature.
- Reduce my use of technology on the Sabbath.
- Spend at least half an hour in silence.

1. _____

2. _____

This year, Lord, help me to:

**(pick at least two of the following goals, or
come up with your own actions)**

- Make a plan to read the entire Bible.
- Make Sabbath meals with local or organic foods.
- Invite someone to share a Sabbath meal.
- Read a book aloud on the Sabbath.
- Abstain from criticism and worry on the Sabbath and refocus on God's grace when such thoughts enter my mind.
- Write a letter of appreciation.
- Gradually eliminate my use of technology on the Sabbath.
- Avoid driving on my day of rest, except to church.
- Avoid eating out and buying things on the Sabbath.

1. _____

2. _____

"Dear heavenly Father, thank You for the opportunity of work and the gift of rest. Help me to remember the days of bondage in Egypt and Pharaoh's refusal to allow the Hebrew people time for worship and rest in You. Protect me from the self-imposed bondage of an unholy 24/7 life. Instead, teach me to honor and treasure the gift of Sabbath rest. May the Sabbath restore my soul and draw me closer to You. May it help me to resist the incessant call of the material world the remaining six days of the week. I thank You, God, for Your desire to spend time with me on this holy day. Amen."

Digging Deeper: *What Scripture Says About Rest*

God set the pattern for humanity: Work six days and rest the seventh. "And on the seventh day God finished the work that he had done, and he rested on the seventh day from all the work that he had done." *(Genesis 2:2)*

The seventh day is a time of holy rest. "So God blessed the seventh day and hallowed it, because on it God rested from all the work that he had done in creation." *(Genesis 2:3)*

This shared pattern of work and rest is a tie that binds humankind to God, and God to humankind. "[H]allow my Sabbaths that they may be a sign between me and you, so that you may know that I the LORD am your God." *(Ezekiel 20:20)*

As if he knew that we would easily forget the gift of Sabbath rest, God urges us to "remember" the Sabbath and to extend its blessing to every living creature. "Remember the Sabbath day, and keep it holy. Six days you shall labor and do all your work. But the seventh day is a Sabbath to the LORD your God; you shall not do any work—you, your son or your daughter, your male or female slave, your livestock, or the alien resident in your towns. For in six days the LORD made heaven and earth, the sea, and all that is in them, but rested the seventh day; therefore the LORD blessed the Sabbath day and consecrated it." *(Exodus 20:8–11)*

Those who keep the Sabbath will be rewarded abundantly. "[A]ll who keep the Sabbath, and do not profane it, and hold fast my covenant—these I will bring to my holy mountain, and make them joyful in my house of prayer." *(Isaiah 56:6–7)*

Sabbath rest is a gift that should be treasured. "Then he said to them, 'The Sabbath was made for humankind, and not humankind for the Sabbath.'" *(Mark 2:27)*

It is a gift that cannot be rescinded—a permanent blessing that ties us to God. "So then, a Sabbath rest still remains for the people of God; for those who enter God's rest also cease from their labors as God did from his." *(Hebrews 4:9–10)*

Observing the Sabbath will bring us delight in the Lord like nothing else. "If you refrain from trampling the Sabbath, from pursuing your own interests on my holy day; if you call the Sabbath a delight and the holy day of the LORD honorable; if you honor it, not going your own ways, serving your own interests, or pursuing your own affairs; then you shall take delight in the LORD, and I will make you ride upon the heights of the earth." *(Isaiah 58:13–14)*

It is a reminder that all of "our" time belongs to God, not just on the Sabbath, but every day throughout our lives. "My times are in your hands." *(Psalm 31:15)*

It is a time to lay down our burdens and find peace. "Come to me, all you that are weary and are carrying heavy burdens, and I will give you rest." *(Matthew 11:28)*

Adapted with permission from *The Gospel According to the Earth: Why the Good Book Is a Green Book* by Matthew Sleeth (HarperOne, 2010)

Session 8
Work

Session Summary

❝ *Always give yourselves fully to the work of the Lord, because you know that your labor in the Lord is not in vain.* **❞**

—1 Corinthians 15:58 (NIV)

A majority of our life is spent at work. The availability of work, and the health and opportunity to do work are blessings. Work itself is a good thing; God created us to work.

Humanity's first work assignment is found in the second chapter of Genesis; we are told to be gardeners—men and women together, protecting and tending the earth. This mandate applies whether we're tilling the soil or shopping in the grocery store.

God's intent for humankind to care for the planet and all its creatures doesn't have an expiration date. It didn't run out at the Fall or at the cross; God's instructions for Adam and Eve stretch through time to our day and age—and beyond.

All of us were meant to be caretakers. It is the work of our lives, but what does it mean to be stewards of the earth at a computer, on the construction site, or down at the plant? Few of us are shepherds, farmers, or gardeners by profession.

Irrespective of our particular occupation, God is calling *all* of us to take better care of the planet. We must examine our work in light of the gifts we have been given and the biblical call to care for the earth. As a result of this self-examination, some of us may feel called to new work; most of us will find new ways of getting to and from work, purchasing materials, delivering goods and services, and performing tasks in ways that better demonstrate our love for God and what He's made. No activity is exempt; nearly every task can be made "greener." This is not something we can delegate. It will require work.

However, this work is best done together. Workplaces are communities where we can share our unique gifts and talents in service of God to benefit others. We can create a ripple effect and show what Christians are *for*, serving with a joyful attitude as caretakers of God's green earth.

Reflections on Work

For seven years after I graduated from high school, I worked as a carpenter. One of my favorite memories as a builder was framing up houses in the fall. The air was crisp and clear, my body was still strong and capable of working hard, and there was something that felt good about working with other people.

At the end of each day we would put away our tools and survey the progress we had made. While the task of sawing each individual rafter to the right length and angle might seem mundane, seeing entire walls, ceilings, and roofs emerge in what used to be open air is nothing short of miraculous. It's rewarding to build something in the place of nothing; we can only imagine how God must have enjoyed the process of creating a home for all His creatures—this remarkably diverse planet we call Earth.

In the beginning, after creating the earth and waters and skies, God placed Adam in the Garden of Eden. Adam had only one boss, and this boss gave Adam a pretty interesting assignment: God told Adam to tend and protect the garden.

As caretaker of the entire earth, Adam was responsible for helping new things grow and flourish. He was steward of all creation. And in those first days, Adam was 100 percent connected with God in his every effort. This is how God intended work to be: done in humility, in service of Him.

Humanity has strayed from this original mandate to tend and protect: instead, our desire for comfort and convenience has caused much harm to the planet. Yet physical work can provide health and meaning to our lives. While the disciples sailed, Jesus walked across the Sea of Galilee to meet them. He picked grain. He washed his disciples' feet. Work was not beneath him. He thought no physical labor was undignified. The washing of feet is a sign that God is willing to stoop low and to work to save us. Shouldn't we be willing to work with all our hearts, minds, souls, and strength to help save His creation?

—**Dr. Matthew Sleeth**

Session Notes: Work

As you watch the eighth session film, **Work**, use the following page to jot down notes, thoughts, and questions.

Hope Begins with a Changed Heart

From the very beginning, the Bible teaches us that work is a good activity. Why has "work" gotten a bad reputation? Do we work just to buy things, or does work have other value besides a paycheck?

66 *The availability of work, and the health and opportunity to do work, are blessings.* **99**

—*Dr. Matthew Sleeth*

2

How is work a blessing? How does too much or too little work affect our mental, physical, emotional, and spiritual health?

---

66 *We were all meant to be gardeners. It is the work of our lives. But what does it mean to be gardeners at a computer, in a cubicle, on the construction site, or down at the plant?* **99**

—*Dr. Matthew Sleeth*

3

How can you be a better "gardener" at work? How do you—or can you— better care for and protect the parts of God's creation entrusted to your care?

4 *« The idea that the service to God should have only to do with a church altar, singing, reading, sacrifice, and the like is without doubt but the worst trick of the devil. How could the devil have led us more effectively astray than by the narrow conception that service to God takes place only in a church and by the works done therein.... The whole world could abound with the services to the Lord ... not only in churches but also in the home, kitchen, workshop, field. »*

—*Martin Luther (1483–1546)*

What qualities make work "godly"? Are these qualities found in your current work at home or the office? Do you perceive your daily work as service to God?

5 *« 'To dress it and keep it.'*
That, then, was to be our work.
Alas! What work have we set ourselves instead?
How have we ravaged the garden instead of kept it— »

—*John Ruskin (1819–1900)*

In our commerce and workplaces, how have we "ravaged the garden"? Give examples.

Dr. Sleeth compares Paul and Zacchaeus and the effect of their conversion experiences on their line of work. For Paul, his conversion resulted in a complete career change. In Zacchaeus' case, his occupation didn't change, but how he performed his work changed radically. How about you? Have you felt a call from God to change your work? If so, in what direction do you feel God leading? How does knowing and following Jesus affect how you do your work?

6

7 *" Where we find buildings that are ugly, furniture ill-made, doors that do not close properly, vines and fruits trees clumsily pruned, materials and fodder going to waste, the lack of skill and care which these things represent might simply be the fruit of a wrong attitude toward work itself. "*

—*Thomas Merton (1915–1968), The Silent Life*

Shoddy work ultimately is a form of waste. Can you give an example of when bad planning or poor quality was wasteful in the long haul? How does accountability to God help us grow more conscientious in our work?

Dr. Sleeth states: "Irrespective of your particular job, God is calling all of us to take better care of the planet. This is not something we can delegate.... There's no activity that a business is involved in that can't be made greener."

8

What are some ways you can modify your work activities—and the activities of your business, company, or organization—to better care for creation? Give examples.

❝ *As gardeners we are involved in a multi-generational project. That's why we believe in life—because our work goes forth for generations, leaving a legacy.* **❞**

9

—*Dr. Matthew Sleeth*

What legacy is your work leaving for future generations? What legacy do you want to leave?

A Changed Heart = A Changed Life

My first real job after college was as a technical writer at a Department of Energy research facility. My office was in a trailer that had been salvaged from the 1977 Johnstown, Pennsylvania, flood. The orange carpet was perpetually damp and the air had a distinctive, old-mold smell.

Six months later I was promoted to the administrative offices—a bunch of newly manufactured trailers linked together to create one large maze of cubicles. If you've ever gotten a whiff of a "new car smell," multiply that tenfold and you'll have a sense of the air we inhaled eight hours a day. At twenty-one, I wasn't particularly concerned about the long-term health consequences of indoor air pollution or the number of trees we used editing multiple drafts of long bureaucratic reports—I was just grateful to have a job that paid the bills.

My colleagues were mostly engineers, trying to find ways of burning fossil fuels—particularly coal—more cleanly and efficiently. Three decades later, scientists and engineers are still searching for the holy grail of "clean coal" (a term many now consider an oxymoron). Despite good intentions, my work at the research facility probably did more environmental harm than good—using lots of resources with little or no benefit to the planet.

When I switched from technical writing to teaching English, the results of my work seemed more straightforward. It wasn't until I taught at the boarding school, however, that my advocacy for health, environmental, and money-saving changes went into high gear. By then, Matthew had left medicine, and we had significantly downscaled our lifestyle. After successfully implementing so many changes at home, I now felt it was time to help lighten the footprint of my workplace.

During my first contract meeting with my boss, I explained that taking care of the planet was my passion. He politely told me that it was not his.

It took a few years, but—despite some initial resistance—the workplace gradually became greener: we began to use recycled paper in all copiers and offices; set double-sided printing as the default in printers; installed LED bulbs in exit signs; added motion detectors for interior lighting; installed dimmers in rooms with natural light; added Dumpster-sized recycling receptacles for paper, glass, plastics, and metal; greatly reduced the use of Styrofoam in the cafeteria; and began composting food waste.

The key to success was working with the system—and forming a "green team"—to make the workplace healthier, more environmentally responsible, and more cost-effective.

The typical office worker uses a quarter of a ton (500 pounds) of materials in a year, including ten thousand pieces of copy paper.

With a little imagination, any field can be made more green: office workers can arrange a rideshare board, hairdressers can compost hair clippings, landscapers can use native plants, house cleaners can switch to natural cleaning products, restaurants can purchase locally grown food. Starting a green task force that recommends ways to save the company money while saving the earth and creating a healthier work environment will result in a win-win-win bottom line.

Can it be challenging to initiate changes at work? Yes. Will you face obstacles? Definitely. The great thing about changes in the workplace is that they have the potential to make a big difference. Not only can you reduce the environmental impact of the entire company, but your example can also influence coworkers' behavior at home.

When colleagues ask why you are going green, don't hesitate to say that your faith is a primary motivation. By adopting good stewardship practices, you are sharing your love of the Creator—and becoming a living testimony through your behavior. Think of creation care as a mission field—an opportunity for us to grow ever closer to the example set by Jesus—and a tangible way to share His perfect love with those who have fewer resources than we do.

—Nancy Sleeth

Adapted with permission from *Go Green, Save Green: A Simple Guide to Saving Time, Money, and God's Green Earth* (Tyndale, 2009)

Good Steward Action Plan: Work

Instructions

1. Pick two or more new actions from the suggested lists to commit to today, this week, this month, and this year—or come up with your own ideas for serving God and caring for the earth through your work.
2. Go to blessedearth.org. and join our community of Good Stewards. Explore the website to find additional ideas for saving energy and becoming a better steward of God's creation.
3. We will send you encouragement throughout the year and help you stay on track with your goals. As God's fellow workers, we're all in this together, so share your journey. Let us know what was easy, what was more difficult, and inspire others with your story!

Today, Lord, help me to:

(pick at least two of the following goals, or come up with your own actions)

- Pray that my work habits would reflect Christ's love for people and creation.
- Activate my computer's standby mode setting.
- Set my printer's default setting to double-sided printing.
- Use draft mode for printing when documents aren't yet final.
- Bring my own coffee mug to work instead of using disposable cups.
- Turn off my computer, printer, and peripherals when I leave work for the day.
- Turn off the lights when I leave my workspace; work under natural light when possible.

1. _____

2. _____

This week, Lord help me to:

(pick at least two of the following goals, or
come up with your own actions)

- Carpool with someone who lives and works near me; use public transportation, walk, or bike to work when possible.
- Print documents only when necessary.
- Reuse envelopes and packaging products in the office.
- Take the stairs instead of the elevator.
- Give up two restaurant or cafeteria lunches; bring a lunch from home in reusable containers instead.
- Investigate ink cartridge and e-waste recycling opportunities.
- Set up a recycling box and bring home the recyclables myself if there is no recycling program at work.

1. _____

2. _____

❝ *I believe that God wants us to live in tension, constantly working to make decisions that bring us closer to Him. Anybody could point at me and say 'hypocrite' regarding many aspects of my work and home life. One area that we currently struggle with is transportation. I need to travel to churches to share our message, and try to do it in the most environmentally responsible way—grouping events geographically, driving in an efficient car, carpooling, etc. But it would be better if I did not have to travel at all.*

"We are all on this creation care journey together. If we can do a little more each year, we're on the right path. **❞**

—*Matthew Sleeth*

This month, Lord, help me to:

(pick at least two of the following goals, or
come up with your own actions)

- Ask my employer about the possibility of telecommuting one day a week or working a four-day week.
- Set up a recycling program at work, or help support one already in place.
- Post reminders beside light switches to turn off lights when leaving the room.
- Switch to refillable pens, pencils, ink cartridges, etc.
- Dress for the weather in my office to minimize heat or AC use.
- Set up a rideshare board to encourage others to carpool.

1. _____

2. _____

_____

❝ *The essence of our work as humans must be that it is done in conscious reliance on God's power, and in conscious quest of God's pattern of excellence, and in deliberate aim to reflect God's glory.* **❞**

—*John Piper, Don't Waste Your Life*

This year, Lord, help me to:

(pick at least two of the following goals, or come up with your own actions)

- Help my employer to recycle electronics.
- Bring live plants to work to improve indoor air quality.
- Start or join a "green team" at your workplace.
- Facilitate an energy audit of the workplace and work to implement recommended changes.
- Help my employer to switch to nontoxic cleaning supplies.
- Encourage my employer to turn the thermostat up three or more degrees in warm months and down three or more degrees in cold months.

1. _____

2. _____

Adapted with permission from *Go Green, Save Green: A Simple Guide to Saving Time, Money, and God's Green Earth* (Tyndale, 2009) and www.blessedearth.org.

❝ *Dear heavenly Father, help me today to honor You in my work and to exercise wisdom and discernment when using the resources You put into my care. Fill my heart with gratitude for Your daily provisions and help me take personal action to become a better steward at work. Teach me to become a humble servant and to lead others toward responsible environmental stewardship through the way I live and work. Give me courage and perseverance as I learn to care for Your creation. Strengthen my desire to make You Lord over every area of my life. Amen.* **❞**

Digging Deeper: *What Scripture Says About Work*

God's first commandment to man was to tend and keep the earth.
"The LORD God took the man and put him in the garden of Eden to till it and keep it." *(Genesis 2:15)* The Bible repeatedly affirms that work is not a result of the Fall, but rather a dignified and essential part of God's created order.

The relationship between man and the land is antagonistic because of our sin. "When you till the ground, it will no longer yield to you its strength!" *(Genesis 4:12)*

Indeed, because of our sin, all of creation suffers. "We know that the whole creation has been groaning in labor pains." *(Romans 8:22; see also Genesis 6:7; Leviticus 26; Deuteronomy 11:13–17)*

God wants us to use the land, not abuse it. "Is it not enough for you to feed on the good pasture, but you must tread down with your feet the rest of your pasture? When you drink of clear water, must you foul the rest with your feet?" *(Ezekiel 34:18)*

God wants us to work for the benefit of others, not focused on our money but on our usefulness. "Do not work for the food that perishes, but for the food that endures for eternal life." *(John 6:27)*

If done in harmony with His creation, God promises that our work will yield great benefits. One reward of hard work is wisdom and respect. The wife described in Proverbs 31 "looks well to the ways of her household, and does not eat the bread of idleness.... She opens her mouth with wisdom, and the teaching of kindness is on her tongue." *(Proverbs 31:27, 26; see also Proverbs 12:11; 13:4; 14:4; 31:10–27)*

Work both strengthens and affirms the reality of our faith. When we hang laundry on the line, or recycle, our love for God is made tangible through daily acts of humble service. "For just as the body without the spirit is dead, so faith without works is also dead." *(James 2:26)*

One of the greatest rewards of work is that it allows us to share with others. "[R]ather let them labor and work honestly with their own hands, so as to have something to share with the needy." *(Ephesians 4:28; see also Proverbs 9:1–6)*

Indeed, God wants us to find pleasure in work because dignified labor is part of His plan for creation. "There is nothing better for mortals than to eat and drink, and find enjoyment in their toil. This also, I saw, is from the hand of God." *(Ecclesiastes 2:24; see also Ecclesiastes 5:12)*

Adapted with permission from *The Gospel According to the Earth: Why the Good Book Is a Green Book* by Matthew Sleeth (HarperOne, 2010)

Additional Study: *Matthew 6:25, 32–33; Matthew 11:28; 1 Corinthians 15:58; 1 Thessalonians 4:11–12; 2 Thessalonians 3:10–12.*

A Meditation on the Lord's Prayer

WHAT ARE WE SET ON EARTH FOR? Say, to toil;
Nor seek to leave thy tending of the vines
For all the heat o' the day, till it declines,
And Death's mild curfew shall from work as soil.
God did anoint thee with His odorous oil,
To wrestle, not to reign; and He assigns all
Thy tears over, like pure crystal lines,
for younger fellow-workers of the soil to wear for amulets. So others shall
Take patience, labor, to their heart and hand from thy hand
And thy heart and thy brave cheer,
And God's grace fructify through thee
To the least flower with a brimming cup may stand,
And share its dew-drop with another near.

—Elizabeth Barrett Browning (1806–1861)

Session 9
Give

Session Summary

❝ It is more blessed to give than to receive. ❞

—Acts 20:35 (NIV)

When we take only what we need, we often find that we have far more resources at our disposal than we can consume for ourselves. When we steward our time and work to provide for our needs, taking what we need for today and trusting God with tomorrow, most of us have an abundance left over. And we're faced with a choice: store up treasure for ourselves here on earth … or give it away.

The first story of giving in the Bible is that of Cain and Abel. These are the sons of Adam and Eve. Abel brings the very best of what he has as an offering to God. In contrast, Cain holds back. And as a result, sin pours into his life, damaging his relationship with God and his brother.

Right from the start we are taught something fundamental about the human heart: lack of generosity keeps us from God.

It doesn't matter if this is in church, at work, or at home: holding back is wrong. It's one of the greatest affronts to the spirit of God. Give without thinking, give the best, and you're on the right track. The most winsome trait of a follower of Christ is generosity.

If we start with the premise that our God is a generous God, a God who gives without thought of balancing accounts, then how should we act if we are made in God's image and called to imitate Him?

Scripture is clear: hoarding is bad; giving is good—for us, for our neighbors, and for God's green earth.

Reflections on Give

Two of my dearest friends, Geoff and Sherry, bought a house in the poorest section of Lexington, Kentucky. They are two of the most generous people I know, living out their love of Christ through daily acts of kindness toward the people in their community.

They've started an urban garden, served on the low-income housing board, and remained extremely active in the neighborhood association. Geoff regularly helps with refugees who come to Lexington from war-torn countries and Sherry is working to start an urban orchard and outdoor classroom.

Both are deeply devoted to their neighbors. Hospitality is a top priority in their home, and they nearly always have at least one non-family member living with them. People stop by for dinner and stay for a month. They are listed as the next of kin for several elderly neighbors and have been called to the hospital in the middle of the night to help make major life decisions. Neighbors knock on their door and unload their troubled lives.

Sherry recently told me about a severely mentally challenged man who shows up at their door fairly regularly, often before dawn. He thinks he is the godfather of their six-year-old son, and Geoff and Sherry treat him as if he really is Isaac's godfather, inviting him in for a cup of coffee before the birds are even awake.

I know we are not supposed to envy, but I do. I envy the way they dare to care, as our Lord Jesus did, for those who have been marginalized and abandoned.

Geoff and Sherry have lived for the last decade on a modest income, but they are rich beyond measure. I have seen them share their income with a young couple who had even less then they did. Their selfless, joyous generosity has taught me much about God's economy, where it truly is better to give than receive.

—*Nancy Sleeth*

Adapted with permission from *Go Green, Save Green: A Simple Guide to Saving Time, Money, and God's Green Earth* (Tyndale, 2009)

Session Notes: Give

As you watch the ninth session film, **Give**, use the following page to jot down notes, thoughts, and questions.

Hope Begins with a Changed Heart

1 **❝** *After we have rested, then comes work. And after we have worked, we have the fruits of our labor. This can literally be fruits or vegetables, but more often the harvest is money or expertise.* **❞**

—*Dr. Matthew Sleeth*

What do you do with the first fruits of your labor? Do you pay the bills first, and then give, or give first and then pay the bills?

2 **❝** *Our lack of generosity keeps us from God. It doesn't matter if this is in church, or at work, or at home. Holding back is wrong. It's one of the greatest affronts to the spirit of God.* **❞**

—*Dr. Matthew Sleeth*

In what sense does a lack of generosity keep us from God? Why is it wrong? How is it an "affront" to God?

Dr. Sleeth asks, "If we start with the premise that our God is a generous God, a God who gives without thought of balancing accounts—then how should we act if we are made in God's image?" In Ephesians, we're specifically called to be "imitators of God." Do your giving habits reflect God's—His extravagant generosity? If not, what is holding you back?

3

❝ *Give without thinking, give the best, and you're on the right track.* **❞**

—*Dr. Matthew Sleeth*

4

In what circumstances do you tend to "give without thinking"? When do you give your best? When do you tend to hold back?

5   **66** *In the Old Testament, we learn about the tithe, or the giving of 10 percent to help the widow, the orphan, the refugee, and the work of the church. But in our land of plenty, what is the right amount to give away today? How do we separate our wants from our needs?* **99**

—*Dr. Matthew Sleeth*

How do you define your "needs"? How has God demonstrated His faithfulness to provide for you? What percent of your money do you believe God is calling you to give toward helping others? How do you determine the "right amount" to give?

❝ *Do not store up for yourselves treasure on earth, where moth and rust destroy, and where thieves break in and steal. But store up for yourselves treasure in heaven, where moth and rust do not destroy, and where thieves do not break in and steal. For where your treasure is, there your heart will be also.* **❞**

—Matthew 6:19–21 (NIV)

Jesus teaches that the way we spend our resources serves as a reflection of our hearts. God sees our true motivations. He knows that if our hearts are focused on storing treasures in heaven, we won't worry about the things we "want" on this earth. When we use the resources God's given us with hearts focused on storing our treasures in heaven, we're more concerned with loving God, loving His creation, and loving our neighbors than on our own comfort on earth—we're leading both spiritual and environmentally sustainable lives. Right now, today, you are an investor. Where are you investing? How do your spending habits reveal the priorities of your heart?

7 *And [Jesus] looked up and saw the rich putting their gifts into the treasury. And He saw a certain poor widow putting in two small copper coins. And He said, 'Truly I say to you, this poor widow put in more than all of them; for they all out of their surplus put into the offering; but she out of her poverty put in all that she had to live on.*

—*Luke 21:1–4 (NASB)*

Dr. Sleeth says he has heard of many people who have gone into debt because of greed, poor planning, or unforeseen disasters, but "not one story of a person or couple going broke from having overdrawn an account to feed the poor, or clothe the naked, or take in the orphan." What do behaviors that lead us into debt say about our priorities? What does generosity teach us about living in faith?

8 Dr. Sleeth observes, "Money is not the only valuable thing that we can give away. One area that costs nothing but we are all too often stingy with is encouragement and compliments." When was the last time you gave a compliment or sent a note of encouragement? Name some specific ways you can be more generous with positive words.

Tending and protecting the planet requires sacrifice. Explain how living more simply, taking less for ourselves, and conserving resources is a form of giving. In what sense are recycling, adjusting the thermostat, and using public transportation acts of sacrificial giving? In what ways are you giving sacrificially? How could you give more? How can living this way bring us closer to Christ's generous example?

ff *But whoever has the world's goods, and beholds his brother in need and closes his heart against him, how does the love of God abide in him?* **ff**

—*1 John 3:17 (NASB)*

How is taking care of the planet a form of giving?

A Changed Heart = A Changed Life

One way our family has learned to give is by making "our" home a center for mission and ministry. Our first mission was to recycle.

Four out of every five pieces of junk mail are not recycled. Junk mail fills 340,000 garbage trucks a year, all bound for landfills.

The paper in these mountains of un-asked-for mail comes from trees, the dyes are chemicals, and the dioxin created in the papermaking process contaminates our freshwater supplies so that I can't eat a fish from the river that runs by our house without risking cancer. Recycling aluminum cans, for example, helps prevent mountains from being leveled and prevents water supplies from being contaminated. Recycling is a simple way for my family to give back to global neighbors.

Another way our family decided to give is by not buying products made from rainforest timber. How does refraining from buying a teak chair constitute "giving"? As the demand for disposable chopsticks and teak furniture grows, the trees in the third world are cut down, the topsoil washes away, the streams dry up, and impoverished villagers flee to cities where childhood prostitution, exploitation, gangs, violence, and corruption are the norm.

Not using throwaway chopsticks can keep an eight-year-old out of a brothel in Indonesia.

Our "best buys" are simply to forgo a purchase altogether. In general, we've come to realize that if we've lived without it for the first twenty-five years of our marriage, we can probably do without it forever. Buying less is not only good for the planet, it frees up money for us to give to others.

Sometimes, however, it's worth paying more. If the product is cheaply made and might easily break, it represents another kind of waste. Also, unbeknownst to most Americans, one consequence of our demand for ever-lower prices is that many companies now use underpaid labor to keep costs down in a competitive market. As followers of Jesus, it's worth paying a premium for Fair Trade certified products to ensure the well-being of our global neighbors.

These are simple "sacrifices" to make. When I read Butler's *Lives of Martyrs*, I marvel. Those heroes of God were stabbed, mauled, impaled, dismembered, and burned as a witness to their love of Jesus. Their sacrifice did not drive others away from Christ but toward him. Roman guards in charge of these martyrs were converted on the spot and gave up their own lives.

Now, hanging clothing on the line, giving up plastic wrap, and changing the light bulbs are hardly the equivalent of being burned alive as a human torch to light up one of Nero's parties. But even today, people, like the Roman guards, are drawn to anyone who believes in something enough to change his lifestyle.

Our new house has no clothes dryer, garbage disposal, or garage, but it's a place of sharing and prayer. We happily have several dozen people into our house for neighborhood potluck dinners, student cookouts, and faith groups. I do not think that anyone can say what the "right" size house is; compared to homes I have visited on medical missions in Honduras, our current house is indefensibly large. We still live better than nearly everyone else on the planet, and we are looking to downsize again. Each time we divest ourselves of possessions, we have fewer earthly things that bind us.

None of these changes we've made will earn us entrance into heaven, but they do two important things for our souls: they connect us with the family of humanity around the globe, and, more importantly, they bring us closer to the heart of God. If He asks us to give up everything we have and follow Him, as He asked the rich young ruler, I now know with certainty that each member of my family would gladly do so. This lack of attachment to material things brings us priceless freedom to give without thinking whenever we hear God's call.

—*Dr. Matthew Sleeth*

Adapted with permission from *Serve God, Save the Planet* (Zondervan, 2007)

Good Steward Action Plan: Give

Instructions

1. Pick two or more new actions from the suggested lists to commit to today, this week, this month, and this year—or come up with your own way to imitate the generosity of our gracious God.
2. Go to blessedearth.org. and join our community of Good Stewards. Explore the website to find additional ideas for saving energy and becoming a better steward of God's creation.
3. We will send you encouragement throughout the year and help you stay on track with your goals. As followers of Christ, we're all in this together, so share your journey. Let us know what was easy, what was difficult, and inspire others with your story!

Today, Lord, help me to:

(pick at least two of the following goals, or come up with your own actions)

- Memorize one or more Bible verses about giving, such as 2 Corinthians 9:7 or 1 John 3:17.
- Pick up trash in my neighborhood.
- Compliment or encourage someone who goes out of the way to care for God's creation.
- Donate all pocket change.
- Gather up a bag of nonperishable food to drop off at a food pantry.
- Plant trees by donating to Floresta, Eden Reforestation Project, or Heifer International.

1. _____

2. _____

This week, Lord help me to:

**(pick at least two of the following goals, or
come up with your own actions)**

- Bring Fair Trade coffee to work; volunteer to wash coffee mugs.
- Take someone to lunch at a restaurant that uses local or organic foods.
- Offer to run errands for someone when I'm going out.
- Use public transportation.
- Share produce from my garden or extra baked goods with a neighbor.
- Shop at a local business instead of a chain store, or shop at the farmers' market.
- If I have more than I need (TVs, DVD players, computers, tools), give them away so someone can use them NOW, not someday.
- Perform an act of kindness for someone in my neighborhood, like offering to baby-sit so the parents can have a night out, or shoveling a sidewalk.

1. _____

2. _____

_____

❝ *We have one friend who hosts neighborhood gatherings in her backyard the first Sunday of each month. Her house is one of the smallest in the neighborhood, but she and her husband have a big heart for hospitality. The gatherings keep getting bigger, as neighbors invite other neighbors. Over the last year, these Sunday potlucks have become a central part of their family ministry, and a focal point for neighborly sharing. From friends like this, I have learned not to wait for someone else to initiate community activities; if you plan it, they will come.* **❞**

—Nancy Sleeth

This month, Lord, help me to:

(pick at least two of the following goals, or come up with your own actions)

- Walk or bike distances of less than two miles.
- Invite a family in my neighborhood over for dinner.
- Borrow something from a neighbor instead of buying it.
- Advertise and give away an unwanted item on freecycle.com.
- Volunteer at a local soup kitchen, thrift shop, or community service organization.
- Talk to my local officials to find out what my town is doing to protect the environment and how I can help.

1. _____

2. _____

This year, Lord, help me to:

(pick at least two of the following goals, or come up with your own actions)

- Commit to tithing my income.
- Start an eco-team in my neighborhood or join the local chapter of a national conservation group.
- Commit to personally supporting a ministry.
- Help a student with tuition.
- Greet new families within a week of their arrival to the neighborhood.
- Adopt a refugee family that has recently moved to my area.
- Help plan a community garden or garage sale.
- Lend gladly to friends and neighbors when they ask to borrow.
- Coordinate meals for someone in my neighborhood who has lost a loved one or is ill.
- Line my street with trees, or plant trees in a poor neighborhood.
- Promote bike paths, carpools, and safe sidewalks.
- Talk to my neighbors about purchasing expensive, infrequently used items together.

1. _____

2. _____

Adapted with permission from *Go Green, Save Green: A Simple Guide to Saving Time, Money, and God's Green Earth* (Tyndale, 2009) and www.blessedearth.org.

❝ *Heavenly Father, teach me to act on this truth: everything on earth belongs to You. Help me to graciously give the first fruits of my labor. May these fruits be so pleasing that they winsomely gather others to the great banquet hall of Christ. Grant me an endless supply of love, forgiveness, and the Good News—and teach me to always make room for another at my table. Amen.* **❞**

Digging Deeper: *What Scripture Says About Giving*

God is the giver of all good things, and He knows how to give good gifts. "Every good and perfect gift is from above, coming down from the Father of the heavenly lights." *(James 1:17; see also Psalm 16:2; Matthew 7:7–11)*

God's love is extravagantly generous. He gave His only Son to reconcile all of creation. "For God so loved the world that He gave His only begotten Son …" *(John 3:16)* Jesus came "to give his life as a ransom for many" *(Mark 10:45)*. "For in him all the fullness of God was pleased to dwell, and through him God was pleased to reconcile to himself all things, whether on earth or in heaven, by making peace through the blood of his cross." *(Colossians 1:19–20)*

His gift makes us agents of reconciliation for all of creation. "So if anyone is in Christ, there is a new creation: everything old has passed away; see, everything has become new! All this is from God, who reconciled us to Himself through Christ, and has given us the ministry of reconciliation." *(2 Corinthians 5:17–18)*

God blesses us in order that we might bless others, and is displeased when we hoard resources. Jesus tells a story about a man who's doing really well for himself. He's worked hard, he's made some good investments, and he's accumulated so much wealth he doesn't even have a place to store it all. God's really blessed him. So he builds himself a bigger barn and takes an early retirement. God calls the man a fool and takes his life. Jesus tells us, "[T]his is how it will be with anyone who stores up things for himself but is not rich toward God" *(Luke 12:21)*.

Christ's ultimate gift on the cross encourages and empowers us to give up our selfish desires. "For the love of Christ urges us on, because we are convinced that one has died for all; therefore all have died. And he died for all, so that those who live might live no longer for themselves, but for him who died and was raised for them." *(2 Corinthians 5:14–15)* "But whatever was to my profit I now consider loss for the sake of Christ. What is more, I consider everything a loss compared to the surpassing greatness of knowing Christ Jesus my Lord, for whose sake I have lost all things. I consider them rubbish, that I may gain Christ." *(Philippians 3:7–8)*

Instead of seeking our own interests, we are to serve the interests of others. "Do nothing out of selfish ambition or vain conceit, but in humility consider others better than yourselves. Each of you should look not only to your own interests, but also to the interests of others. Your attitude should be the same as that of Christ Jesus." *(Philippians 2:3–5, NIV)*

God desires for us to act justly and live humbly. "He has showed you, O man, what is good. And what does the LORD require of you? To act justly and to love mercy and to walk humbly with your God." *(Micah 6:8, NIV)*

If we can simply give up our pride, then God will heal the land. "When I shut up the heavens so that there is no rain ... if my people, who are called by my name, will humble themselves and pray and seek my face and turn from their wicked ways, then will I hear from heaven and will forgive their sin and will heal their land." *(2 Chronicles 7:13–14, NIV; see also Isaiah 58)*

Adapted with permission from *The Gospel According to the Earth: Why the Good Book Is a Green Book* by Matthew Sleeth (HarperOne, 2010)

Session 10
Share

Session Summary

❝ Love one another. As I have loved you, so you must love one another. By this, all men will know you are my disciples, if you love one another. ❞

—John 13:34–35 (NIV)

The first-century church was a happening church—a foretaste of heaven. All the believers met together constantly, selling their possessions and sharing everything with those in need. They worshipped together, sharing meals with great joy and generosity. All during this time people were praising God and enjoying each other's company. And each day new members were added to their gatherings.

It's quite a picture—people who see church not as a building but as a way of life. What a far cry from our concept of church today! As a society we long for community; we long for a sense of belonging. So how did we get from church as described in the Bible where joyful generosity was the norm to where we are today?

Today, we live in a country that makes up just 5 percent of the world's population, and yet we use 25 percent of the world's energy. We use roughly half the world's paper. Is it possible to conserve resources, and at the same time build fellowship? Yes! The trick is to be more like the first-century church. More simply, the trick is to be more like Jesus.

I believe part of the reason we buy so much and we own so much is because it's easier to remain isolated and independent than to share. As Americans, we not only define ourselves by the things we own, but we take pride in not having to ask for anything. Individualism and independence are some of our culture's supreme values. By sharing and practicing hospitality, we return to "church" as God intended it to be.

Church is a verb—a dynamic, active community engaged in loving service—not a static noun. Love one another, and by this, all of humanity will know you follow Jesus.

Reflections on Share

Sharing is about generosity, and generosity is the engine of the church. In his book Life Together, *Dietrich Bonhoeffer—the brilliant German theologian who died a martyr in a Nazi concentration camp—talks about the grace that God affords us by allowing us to live in community with fellow believers. Bonhoeffer suggests that one of greatest blessings one can have is life together.*

As the first-century church discovered, life together is not always easy. When you "do church," there will be friction and controversy. We have all been raised in an environment of hyper individuality and must actively practice the skills that allow us to live together.

God's church, as His bride and the body of Christ, is meant to be a community of people who care for one another and serve as the hands and feet of Jesus in the world. The church community is a natural place to give, borrow, and lend. Scripture is explicit about the need to share: "[D]o not refuse anyone who wants to borrow from you" (Matthew 5:42).

Church also offers opportunities for extending hospitality. I did not grow up in a home that offered much in the way of hospitality, and I have learned much from those who open their homes to me—and from my wife, Nancy. She seems to have a natural gift for making people comfortable. Over a recent week we had thirty-nine people over for dinner in five different groups. Hospitality is not always easy, but it's a great way to build community.

One of the groups was comprised of neighbors—many of whom are training to become pastors. We have started to work together in an intentional way to share tools, a garden, and automobiles. No neighborhood need own more than one chainsaw, power saw, copy of a particular movie, or extension ladder.

God owns the earth, and everything on it. By learning to work cooperatively, the church honors God, our ever-gracious Host.

—Dr. Matthew Sleeth

Adapted with permission from *The Gospel According to the Earth: Why the Good Book Is a Green Book* (HarperOne, 2010)

Session Notes: Share

As you watch the tenth session film, **Share**, use the following page to jot down notes, thoughts, and questions.

Hope Begins with a Changed Heart

1   Dr. Sleeth, paraphrasing the book of Acts, describes the first-century church as follows: "All the believers met together constantly. They sold their possessions and shared everything with those in need. They worshipped together each day, and they met in homes for the Lord's Supper. They shared their meals with great joy and generosity. All during this time people were praising God and enjoying each other's company. And each day new members were added to the group that was being saved."

How is this description of the first-century church different from the church today? In what sense has the church become a building rather than a way of life?

In his book, *The Great Divorce*, C. S. Lewis depicts hell as a place of infinite resources. How can unlimited resources—what most would consider a blessing—lead to undesirable behaviors and outcomes? Give examples.

2

❝ *As a society we long for community. We long for a feeling of belonging.* **❞**

—*Dr. Matthew Sleeth*

3

How does the first-century church differ from our twenty-first century church? How does our culture's focus on wealth and independence pull us away from interdependence and sharing?

4 Christ calls us to "[g]ive to anyone who asks, and don't turn away from those who want to borrow." How do you react when something is returned in less than ideal shape? Or not returned at all? What Christian attitudes must the church bring to borrowing and lending?

Jesus tells us in Luke 12, "From everyone who has been given much, much will be demanded; and from the one who has been entrusted with much, much more will be asked." God shares with us that we might share with others. How does this understanding affect the way you hold on to, let go of, and use the gifts—material goods and personal talents and passions—that He's given to you? Why do you think God has entrusted you with the good things in your life?

5

❝ *But living life together isn't easy. People will always have problems, and there will always be someone who takes more than he gives.* **❞**

6

—*Dr. Matthew Sleeth*

We often shy away from situations that make us less comfortable, that put us out, or cause us to suffer. Discuss examples of when you have given more than you've received, or received more than you've given.

7 Dr. Sleeth observes: "Just as hard as it is to give, it's sometimes even harder to receive." In what sense can asking for or accepting the generosity and hospitality of others be a humbling experience?

8 *" We live in a country that is 5 percent of the world's population, and yet we use a quarter of the world's energy. We use roughly half the world's paper. I believe that it's possible to conserve resources, and at the same time build fellowship. The trick is to be more like the first-century church in the ways that are eternal. "*

—*Dr. Matthew Sleeth*

What are some of the eternal qualities of the first-century church that we should emulate? How can following the example of the-first century church help us conserve resources?

66 *If we are ever able to stop destroying our environment, it will be because person by person we decide, by God's grace, to turn aside from greed and materialism. It will be because we learn that joy and fulfillment come through right relationship with God, neighbor and earth, not an ever-escalating demand for more and more material consumption. Nowhere is that more possible than in local congregations that combine prayer and action, worship and analysis, deep personal love for the Creator and for the Creator's garden.* **99**

—*Dr. Ronald Sider, Professor of Theology and Society,*
Eastern Baptist Theological Seminary

How can the church "foster love for the Creator and for the Creator's garden"? How can the church help us "turn aside from greed and materialism" and pursue a "right relationship with God, neighbor, and earth"?

10 *We have tended to have a good doctrine of redemption, and a bad doctrine of creation. Of course we have paid lip-service to the truth that God is the Creator of all things, but we seem to have been blind to its implications. Our God has been too 'religious,' as if his main interests were worship services and prayer meetings attended by church members. Don't misunderstand me: God does take a delight in the prayers and praises of his people. But now we begin to see him also (as the Bible has always portrayed him) as the Creator, who is concerned for the secular world as well as the church, who loves all men and not Christians only, and who is interested in the whole of life and not merely in religion.*

—*John Stott (1921–), author, preacher, and evangelist*

Name a few activities that your church has been involved in that resemble the first-century church. What ministries would you like to be involved in that would lead to sharing more often?

❝ *The adoption of statements on the environment by church councils and assemblies is important. But unless every local congregation actually carries out sound environmental practices in its buildings and in the homes of the members, these statements are worthless. Care of the earth—our mandate from the Creator—is the responsibility of us all.* **❞**

—*The Reverend Dr. Herbert W. Chilstrom (1931–),*
Bishop, Evangelical Lutheran Church in America

❝ *The challenge before the religious community in America is to make every congregation— every church, synagogue and mosque—truly 'green'—a center of environmental study and action. That is their religious duty.* **❞**

—*James Parks Morton, Dean, Cathedral of St. John the Divine (Episcopal)*

Is your church "green"? What responsibility do you have as an individual member of the body of Christ to be a better steward of creation? What actions are more easily done together? How can you help your church reclaim its God-given responsibility to care for the earth?

A Changed Heart = A Changed Life

A few years ago, Matthew was asked to preach at the church where he grew up. As a result, the church formed five book groups to study *Serve God, Save the Planet*, using the discussion guide to apply stewardship principles to their daily lives at home, work, and church. Out of these book studies, an ongoing creation care group was formed. The group recommended energy-saving actions throughout the church, including changing light bulbs, making recycling bins readily available, and using nondisposable dishes.

One church member bought a dozen cases of light bulbs to share at cost. They sold out immediately, with requests for more bulbs at the next service. The pastor and creation care group also encouraged their building committee to hire a green architect for their new addition. Once the creation care group got going, God opened doors they never dreamed of!

Jesus tells us in Matthew 7 to take the plank out of our own eye before worrying about the speck in someone else's. As sons and daughters of God, we need to clean up our own churchyards first. The changes we make at church show the outside world that we honor the Lord not only in what we say but also in what we do.

D. L. Moody once said, "There are many of us that are willing to do great things for the Lord, but few of us are willing to do the little things." Seemingly small acts, like recycling used announcements, really *do* make a difference. Below are some ideas for getting started:

1. Conduct an energy audit, either through your local utility or a performance contractor. Many church buildings can be made more efficient.
2. Change the lighting in the church to be more energy-efficient.
3. Recycle church bulletins. Encourage people to share bulletins, and reduce the size of the bulletin to fewer pages. Print them on recycled paper.
4. Purchase organic, Fair Trade coffee. Use ceramic mugs instead of disposable cups.
5. Organize a church garden. Soup kitchens, homeless shelters, and local after-school programs will welcome your fresh produce. A church garden is also a great way to engage people who normally don't go to church but are interested in gardening or community service.

6. Start an exchange program. Set up a bulletin board for people to post items they need and items they want to give away. Consider starting a "library" for tools and toys, in addition to books, magazines, and videos.

7. Start a book study or small group on God-centered environmentalism and discuss how group members can reduce their impact on ecosystems.

8. Hold prayer meetings for people affected by environmental changes and natural disasters. Pray for wisdom to know how to help and the strength to carry out God's will.

9. Plant trees native to your region.

10. Organize car pools to and from church. If you have many people coming from one area (such as college students or senior citizens), arrange for a van or bus to take them all to church instead of them driving separately.

11. Share the church building with other organizations. Multiple church congregations can share one church building on Saturdays and Sundays. Soup kitchens and community groups can use the building during the week.

12. Turn off electronic devices in the church when they're not in use.

13. Reduce waste. Set up recycling bins in the church kitchen and throughout the building. Place boxes for cans, plastic, and paper, and bring them to the recycling center on a regular basis.

14. Clean green. Make sure that the cleaning products used at the church are not harmful for the environment and contain no phosphates.

15. Curb clutter. Hold a church yard sale. The fewer things we have, the less distraction in our lives and the more time we have to spend with God. Donate the money raised to church outreach, missions, and worthy charities.

Finally, love one another, for by this the world will know you are Christ's disciples. "Religion that God our Father accepts as pure and faultless is this: to look after orphans and widows in their distress and to keep oneself from being polluted by the world" (James 1:27, NIV). "The only thing that counts is faith expressing itself through love" (Galatians 5:6, NIV).

—Nancy Sleeth

Adapted with permission from *Go Green, Save Green: A Simple Guide to Saving Time, Money, and God's Green Earth* (Tyndale, 2009)

Good Steward Action Plan: Share

Instructions

1. Pick two or more new actions from the suggested lists to commit to today, this week, this month, and this year—or come up with your own way to build a Christlike community.
2. Go to blessedearth.org and join our community of Good Stewards. Explore the website to find additional ideas for saving energy and becoming a better steward of God's creation.
3. We will send you encouragement throughout the year and help you stay on track with your goals. As the body of Christ, we're all in this together, so share your journey. Let us know what was easy, what was difficult, and inspire others with your story!

Today, Lord, help me to:

(pick at least two of the following goals, or come up with your own actions)

- Look online to learn about my denomination's stance on earth stewardship.
- Make a list of people who might be interested in forming a creation care group at my church.
- Visit web resources related to environmentally sustainable churches and download one of the energy-saving guides:

  www.blessedearth.org
  www.creationcare.org
  www.earthministry.org
  www.energystar.gov
  www.theregenerationproject.org
  www.webofcreation.org

1. _____

2. _____

This week, Lord help me to: _____

**(pick at least two of the following goals, or
come up with your own actions)**

- Give someone a ride to church to reduce pollution.
- Talk to friends about how we can help our church be a better steward.
- Walk around the church building and take notes on ways the church could use less resources.
- Make a list of low- or no-cost changes my church community could make to become better stewards.
- See if my church serves Fair Trade coffee; if they don't, research local Fair Trade options and make the switch.
- Pray for people affected by environmental degradation around the world.

1. _____

2. _____

_____

❝ *One encouraging sign of healthy, biblical change in modern church communities has grown out of the new monastic movement. This model of community is centered on a commitment by church members to be involved in one another's everyday life, as well as the lives of their (often poor and urban) neighbors. I've been blessed by friendships with several of these new monastic groups.*

"In addition, home churches are springing up throughout the country. I believe that these home churches are a vital way to fill our longing for community life. In a similar way, within megachurches, small groups act as communities within communities, providing a way to belong, to worship, and to share in the context of an often impersonal world. **❞**

—*Dr. Matthew Sleeth*

This month, Lord, help me to:

(pick at least two of the following goals, or come up with your own actions)

- Encourage my church to conduct an energy audit.
- Ask my pastor to preach a sermon or series on creation care, or invite a guest speaker.
- Start a creation care Bible study group or Sunday school class.
- Talk to the facilities manager at my church about recycling options.
- Ask custodial staff to switch to eco-friendly cleaning products.
- Start a bulletin board or other system where church members can post goods or services to share or give away.

1. _____

2. _____

❝ *First-, second-, and third-century Christians were thought of as outrageous individuals. They were even called rebels, subversives, anti-institution, anti-society, and unpatriotic. But the one thing the watching world gave them credit for was generosity. Their crazy generosity stemmed from their belief that everything belongs to God in the first place, and God never asked us to be stingy on His account.* ❞

—*Dr. Matthew Sleeth*

This year, Lord, help me to:

(pick at least two of the following goals, or come up with your own actions)

- Form an ongoing creation care group in my church or community.
- Switch from disposable to reusable dishes at church.
- Plant trees on church property and in lower-income neighborhoods.
- Avoid use of pesticides and fertilizers on church property.
- Sponsor a series of creation care talks, open to the community.
- Help plan an Earth Day Sunday service and celebration.
- Start a community garden at my church.
- Install a rain collection system for storing water from the roof.
- Adjust thermostats and make other changes to reduce energy usage at my church by at least 10 percent.
- Encourage my church to spend more of its budget each year on giving and reaching out to others in the community.

1. _____

2. _____

Adapted with permission from *The Gospel According to the Earth: Why the Good Book Is a Green Book* (HarperOne, 2010) and www.blessedearth.org

❝ *Dear heavenly Father, You are the Creator, the everlasting God. All I have is Yours. Thank You for entrusting me with the task of caring for Your creation. Forgive me for the times I have neglected the things that are near to Your heart. Take away any self-centeredness and apathy in my thoughts or actions, and help my church to make changes that will protect and preserve the planet. Increase my desire to serve You through caring for Your creation. When I am in need, help me to humbly ask; when asked, may I give without hesitation. Amen.* **❞**

Digging Deeper: *What Scripture Says About Sharing*

Church as Community

One way that the church shows its love is by reaching out to others in our community. "Religion that is pure and undefiled before God, the Father, is this: to care for orphans and widows in their distress, and to keep oneself unstained by the world." *(James 1:27)*

When we take care of those with less than us, we are sharing God's love and, according to Jesus, serving God Himself. "[F]or I was hungry and you gave me food, I was thirsty and you gave me something to drink, I was a stranger and you welcomed me, I was naked and you gave me clothing, I was sick and you took care of me, I was in prison and you visited me…. Truly I tell you, just as you did it to one of the least of these who are members of my family, you did it to me." *(Matthew 25:35–40, NIV)*

Living in harmony often requires us to put the needs of others before our own desires. "Do nothing from selfish ambition or conceit, but in humility regard others as better than yourselves. Let each of you look not to your own interests, but to the interests of others." *(Philippians 2:3–4)*

If we know we can be of help to someone, we must do it, even if it is inconvenient or costly. "Anyone, then, who knows the right thing to do and fails to do it, commits sin." *(James 4:17, NIV)*

The first-century church gives us a model to strive toward. "Now the whole group of those who believed were of one heart and soul, and no one claimed private ownership of any possessions, but everything they owned was held in common." *(Acts 4:32)*

When we intentionally seek to live harmoniously in community, the rewards are abundant. "How very good and pleasant it is when kindred live together in unity!" *(Psalm 133:1)*

Church and Hospitality

Hospitality has always been considered a moral act of neighborliness and mutual aid. From the account of Abraham, Sarah, and the angels *(Genesis 17)* to the story of the widow Zarephath and Elijah *(1 Kings 17)*, we are exhorted to welcome the stranger into our homes and lives.

We are told to love the stranger. The God of Moses is one "who loves the strangers, providing them food and clothing." His people "shall also love the stranger, for you were strangers in the land of Egypt." *(Deuteronomy 10:18–19)*

As a church, we should actively welcome others. "Do not neglect to show hospitality to strangers, for by doing that some have entertained angels without knowing it." *(Hebrews 13:2)* Again, in Paul's letter to the Romans, he exhorts us to "extend hospitality to strangers" *(Romans 12:13)* while Peter tells us to "offer hospitality to one another without grumbling." *(1 Peter 4:8)*

Hospitality is a blessing. A worthy widow is one who has "shown hospitality." *(1 Timothy 5:10)* Job, one of the most godly men who ever lived, "championed the cause of the stranger." *(Job 29:16)*

There are two parts to hospitality: guest and host. Jesus acts as both. He identifies with the stranger—"for I was hungry and you gave me food, I was thirsty and you gave me something to drink, I was a stranger and you welcomed me" *(Matthew 25:35)*—as well as the host who fed five thousand.

Church hospitality should focus on welcoming not only family and friends, but also strangers. "But when you give a banquet, invite the poor, the crippled, the lame, and the blind. And you will be blessed, because they cannot repay you, for you will be repaid at the resurrection of the righteous." *(Luke 14:13–14)*

Ultimately, God the creator and His earth are host to all life. "The earth is the Lord's, and all its fullness, the world and those who dwell therein." *(Psalm 24:1)* We, as good guests, are to share this hospitality with all creatures, great and small, for in our host's "hand is the life of every creature and the breath of all mankind." *(Job 12:9–10)*

Session 11
Teach

Session Summary

> ❮❮ *Teach them to their children, so the next generation might know them—even the children not yet born— and they in turn will teach their own children.* ❯❯
>
> —*Psalm 78:5–6 (NLT)*

Most people have never heard a sermon on Genesis 2:15, God's first job assignment for humanity—the command to tend and protect the earth. They haven't been taught why the Bible says not to cut a fruit tree even in war, or why we are instructed not to muddy the waters. Yet teaching about what the Bible teaches us about caring for the earth and all living things is both a responsibility and a privilege.

How do we teach these lessons? We look to the methods of the ultimate Teacher, Jesus. Sometimes He answers questions with questions. Sometimes He answers directly, like He did when asked how to pray: Pray the Lord's Prayer.

During His ministry on earth, Jesus teaches through stories, rebuke, and encouragement. But perhaps the best way to teach is through example. Too often we want to be the judge and the jury for God, but what Christ is asking us to do is be the witness.

Christ's most memorable lessons are those taught by His life. Jesus made a sacrifice two thousand years ago to pay for my sins, and your sins— the sins of yesterday, today, tomorrow, and forever. And in doing so, He taught us something profound about time: What we do now—even the sacrifices we make—matter for generations to come.

My prayer is that when someone looks at you, they see someone who is humble and meek and willing to sacrifice for the next generation in the same way Christ sacrificed for you.

Reflections on Teach

I know that teachers are not supposed to have favorites, but Josh was a very special boy. At age five, he was extremely inquisitive, honest, and affectionate. He also was obsessed with war. One day, when Josh had just finished drawing yet another exquisitely detailed sword and shield, I asked about this obsession.

Josh was quiet for a full two minutes. A thoughtful boy, he clearly wanted to give me a truthful answer. Finally, he looked me straight in the eyes and replied, "Mrs. Sleeth, it's because boys are boys and girls are girls." A simple yet profound insight for a five-year-old!

I recently finished reading The Idiot *by the Russian novelist Fyodor Dostoevsky. His main character, the Christlike hero Prince Myshkin, has a special relationship with children, just as Jesus did. Young children love the Prince because he is honest and never tries to deceive them. Further, Myshkin has found, as I did with Josh, that "a child can give exceedingly good advice even in the most difficult case."*

I will never forget what I learned from Josh about the differences between boys and girls, and I will never forget the lessons my students taught me each time we went outdoors: turn your face up to the first flakes of snow; watch a butterfly shake its wings dry; lie on your back and imagine shapes in the clouds.

Though we can share knowledge with children, they can teach us something even more valuable: wonderment. Children instinctively understand that nature is precious—more valuable than anything humans can make. They live in the joy of the eternal present, neither dwelling on the past nor fretting about the future.

As adults, we must "train up a child in the way he should go," but at the same time be humble and patient enough to receive instruction, for the "kingdom of heaven belongs to such as these." When it comes to the environment, perhaps the best gift my students gave me was hope.

—*Nancy Sleeth*

Adapted with permission from *Go Green, Save Green: A Simple Guide to Saving Time, Money, and God's Green Earth* (Tyndale, 2009)

Session Notes: Teach

As you watch the eleventh session film, **Teach**, use the following page to jot down notes, thoughts, and questions.

Hope Begins with a Changed Heart

1 *" Teaching about Genesis 2:15 and the hundreds of other green passages in the Bible is a responsibility. We are to pass along the wisdom of the ages to our children, and to their children. Teaching is a biblical calling. "*

—*Dr. Matthew Sleeth*

What steps has your church taken to pass along a love and respect for God's creation?

2 During His life on earth, Jesus taught in many different ways: answering questions with questions, answering questions directly, using illustrations and parables, by experience, through rebuke, through encouragement, and by example. Which of these methods seems to be most memorable? Why?

❝ *We want to be the judge and the jury for God, but what Christ is asking us to do is be the witness.* **❞**

—*Dr. Matthew Sleeth*

How can you be the "witness" for God as you teach about caring for creation? Name some actions you could take that would speak louder than words.

4 Dr. Sleeth admits, "One of my favorite ways of being taught is by being encouraged. I respond so much better to encouragement than discouragement! Jesus was certainly good at encouraging … we need to do the same, whether we're teaching somebody Bible lessons or about recycling." Who can you encourage today? What can you do to affirm someone's efforts to care for creation?

5 Dr. Sleeth suggests, "Saying 'turn off the water' to kids is one thing, but showing them three gallons of water that's wasted while brushing their teeth is quite another." Can you think of other examples of how we can teach about the importance of caring for God's creation through hands-on experience?

The average school-aged child spends less than thirty minutes a week in unstructured play outside. What steps can you take to begin to enjoy and appreciate God's creation on a deeper level?

6

7 ❝ *Reading about nature is fine, but if a person walks in the woods and listens carefully, he can learn more than what is in books, for they speak with the voice of God.* ❞

—*George Washington Carver (early 1860s–1943)*

In what sense does nature "speak with the voice of God"? What will we hear if we listen? What can nature teach us about God's provision, contentment, and peace?

8

** Every one of those beautiful trees that gave syrup, that put on a spectacular color show in the fall, that shaded us in the summer, was a gift to the future from those who came before us. Those people taught by example. And their lining the road with trees is a sermon about faith. **

—*Dr. Matthew Sleeth*

What are some other "sermons about faith" left to us by previous generations? What "sermons about faith" would you like to leave for future generations?

A Changed Heart = A Changed Life

When I worked at a boarding school, I joined a faculty "green team." With the help of two other teachers, we started a paper-recycling program. Students made recycling boxes and asked teachers if they would keep one in each of their rooms. At the end of the week, one of my colleagues arranged to park a school van in a central location. The students in my morning class went around campus offering to collect boxes that had not yet been emptied, and then I drove the van to the recycling center during my lunch break.

The next fall, we expanded our program to include bottles and cans. We obtained blue trash barrels to put around the campus. The industrial arts program drilled a hole in the center of each top, and a student painted "Cans and bottles only" around the hole.

To make the recycling programs a permanent fixture of campus culture, we invited the National Honor Society to take responsibility for bottles and cans. Because there is a five-cent deposit on all beverage containers in the state, the club could collect the redemption money and donate it to a good cause. We then asked the dean of the freshman class if his students would take on paper recycling as an ongoing service project. He agreed, and thereafter responsibility for the recycling program was handed down to each entering freshman class.

Our school also had a senior capstone program. The purpose of the senior capstone was to select an area of personal interest and complete a semester-long research project, "capped" by a practical, service-oriented application. One of my first students wrote a proposal to switch the entire campus to 30-percent recycled paper. When the student demonstrated that it would not cost the school any more money to be more environmentally responsible, the headmaster immediately approved the change. He also promised to switch to the slightly more expensive 100-percent postconsumer recycled content paper once it could be demonstrated that paper usage on campus—and paper costs—had decreased.

At another student's suggestion, the school's head librarian, a member of our faculty green team, switched the default print setting on the library printers from single-sided to double-sided. Paper costs in the library dropped from $9,000 to less than $4,500 in one year—more than twice the savings needed to make a campus switch to 100-percent recycled paper cost neutral.

Another advocate on the green team was a young physics teacher. Working with a nonprofit environmental education program, her class conducted a campus-wide energy audit. The class chose three lighting projects to research and made recommendations in a formal proposal to the administration. All three of the recommended changes—switching to LED lights in exit signs, using motion-detector lighting in selected classrooms, and installing dimmers in the cafeteria where natural lighting was abundant— were immediately approved. The students were commended for proposing changes that were cost effective as well as good for the environment—a lesson not only in physics but also in the rewards of civic involvement.

Even several years later initiatives continue to be proposed and approved—including cutting back on Styrofoam use in the cafeteria and composting cafeteria food waste. The entire waste disposal system was reevaluated, and large glass, plastics, and metal recycling collection sites were installed around campus. As a result, trash production on campus has been reduced by 50 percent.

These students learned by asking questions, researching answers, proposing solutions, and doing. Faculty taught by doing, not just saying. And the entire school became an *example*, with trickle down to students' homes. Instead of being satisfied with what has been accomplished, the school community sees learning as an *ongoing journey*. And the lessons they have learned are being passed along as a *legacy* to future generations of students.

Today, "green" is not only the school's official color—it's also an integral part of the campus culture. The school motto, *Semper Discens* (always learning), applies not only to what we know but also to how we live.

—Nancy Sleeth

Adapted with permission from *Go Green, Save Green: A Simple Guide to Saving Time, Money, and God's Green Earth* (Tyndale, 2009)

Good Steward Action Plan: Teach

Instructions

1. Pick two or more new actions from the suggested lists to commit to today, this week, this month, and this year—or come up with your own way to teach others about creation care.
2. Go to blessedearth.org and join our community of Good Stewards. Explore the website to find additional ideas for saving energy and becoming a better steward of God's creation.
3. We will send you encouragement throughout the year and help you stay on track with your goals. As disciple-makers, we're all in this together, so share your journey. Let us know what was easy, what was difficult, and inspire others with your story!

Today, Lord, help me to:

(pick at least two of the following goals, or come up with your own actions)

- Teach by example.
- Pray that everyone involved in our children's education, myself included, learns to model healthier stewardship practices.
- Make good stewardship choices on behalf of those in my household or under my care.
- Go on a nature walk and invite someone to join me.

1. _____

2. _____

This week, Lord help me to:

(pick at least two of the following goals, or come up with your own actions)

- Continue to teach by example.
- Ask friends about carpooling to school and after-school activities; encourage kids to walk and bike to school more often.
- Call my children's schools to find out if they're using natural cleaning products; if they're not, recommend some options and encourage them to make the switch.
- Find out if the printers in the school's computer lab are set to double-sided default; if they're not, encourage the school to make the change and explain the resource and cost savings involved.
- Encourage kids to take responsibility for caring for God's earth and empower them to share their ideas on how their school can help care for the planet.
- Offer to bring one or more live plants to offices, churches, or school classrooms.
- Donate paper products made from recycled paper to classrooms; educate others about the difference using recycled paper can make.

1. _____

2. _____

_____

ff *If I ever start feeling too complacent in my creation care journey, all I need to do is open my Bible. If we approach God in humility and listen for His voice, His Word is an endless source of learning, growth, and knowledge. God's Word challenges me to ask questions, seek wisdom, and follow the example of our Savior, Jesus Christ.* **ff**

—Matthew Sleeth

This month, Lord, help me to:

(pick at least two of the following goals, or
come up with your own actions)

- Continue to teach by example.
- Spend time outdoors and invite friends and family to join me.
- Call my utility company to find out about energy audits for my children's schools; encourage local schools to conduct an energy audit and make recommended changes.
- Find out if my children's schools have a "green team" and ask to get involved; if they don't, talk to administration about starting one.
- Ask the school librarian if I can help create an environmental display in one of the showcases.
- Talk to youth leaders and Sunday school teachers at church about getting young people involved in the church's creation care efforts; if my church isn't involved in creation care, encourage the younger generation to lead the way.

1. _____

2. _____

This year, Lord, help me to:

(pick at least two of the following goals, or come up with your own actions)

- Continue to teach by example.
- Explain the connection between creation care and loving our neighbors as Jesus commanded when people ask why I'm trying to protect the planet.
- Help local school's "green team" develop a plan of action and get students involved; plan a schoolwide Earth Day celebration.
- Encourage teachers to plan field trips to an organic farm, recycling center, or nature preserve, and volunteer to chaperone the trips.
- Purchase at least half of my children's clothes from secondhand and thrift stores, and develop a network for sharing clothes that my children have outgrown.
- Reuse backpacks instead of buying new ones; encourage kids to donate old or unused backpacks, bags, and clothing to The Salvation Army, Goodwill, or a local homeless ministry.
- Encourage local schools to plant trees, flowers, or a vegetable garden.
- Investigate the possibility of donating leftover perishable cafeteria food to a local nonprofit organization or composting it.

1. _____

2. _____

_____

❝ *My prayer is that, regardless of whether I am teaching about Scripture, or Jesus, or stewardship, I will lead by example. My prayer is that, when I am gone from this world, that I will have done things that will continue to bless the next generation. My prayer is that when someone looks at me, they see someone who is humble and meek and willing to sacrifice. My prayer is that I believe in the next generation in the same way Christ believed in me. Amen.* **❞**

Digging Deeper: *What Scripture Says About Teaching*

Teaching is a biblical calling. "Train a child in the way he should go, and when he is old he will not turn from it." *(Proverbs 22:6)*

We have a responsibility to share what we have learned from God with future generations. "Teach them to their children, so the next generation might know them—even the children not yet born—and they in turn will teach their own children." *(Psalm 78:5-6, NLT)*

As teachers, we must pass along that which is right and good. "I will teach you the way that is good and right." *(1 Samuel 12:23)*

The primary requirement for learning is a longing to be transformed by God. "As a hart longs for flowing streams, so longs my soul for thee, O God. My soul thirsts for God, for the living God. When shall I come and behold the face of God?" *(Psalm 42:1–2)*

All of us have much to learn on the creation care journey. We are all under the power of sin, as it is written: "None is righteous, no, not one." *(Romans 3:10–11)*

God wants us to seek instruction from Him. "[G]uide me in your truth and teach me, for you are God my Savior, and my hope is in you all day long." *(Psalm 25:4–6)*

We need to be quiet in order to learn. "Be still, and know that I am God." *(Psalm 46:10)*

And we need to be patient. "For everything there is a season, and a time for every matter under heaven." *(Ecclesiastes 3:1)*

Part of the journey is eliminating the attitudes that keep us from following God wholeheartedly. "[L]et us also lay aside every weight, and sin which clings so closely, and let us run with perseverance the race that is set before us." *(Hebrews 12:1)*

Just because we can do anything doesn't mean we should. "'All things are lawful for me,' but not all things are helpful. 'All things are lawful for me,' but I will not be enslaved by anything." *(1 Corinthians 6:12)*

We are to pursue wisdom, and learn from those with much to teach us about God and His creation. "He described plant life, from the cedar of Lebanon to the hyssop that grows out of walls. He also taught about animals and birds, reptiles and fish. Men of all nations came to listen to Solomon's wisdom." *(1 Kings 4:33–34)*

We must always remain open to God's teaching and never believe we have it all figured out. "Let my teaching fall like rain and my words descend like dew, like showers on new grass, like abundant rain on tender plants." *(Deuteronomy 32:2)*

Adapted with permission from *The Gospel According to the Earth: Why the Good Book Is a Green Book* by Matthew Sleeth (HarperOne, 2010)

And Nature, the old nurse, took
   The child upon her knee,
Saying: "Here is a story-book
   Thy Father has written for thee."
"Come, wander with me," she said,
   "Into regions yet untrod;
And read what is still unread
   in the manuscripts of God."

—Henry Wadsworth Longfellow (1807–1882),
"The Fiftieth Birthday of Agassiz"

Session 12
Hope

Session Summary

❝** [T]hose who hope in the LORD will renew their strength. They will soar on wings like eagles; they will run and not grow weary, they will walk and not be faint. **❞

—Isaiah 40:31 (NIV)

When Christians talk about "going green" or "saving the planet," they bring something unique to the discussion: hope. Not just hope for a better future someday in heaven, but hope for today through the power of God's Holy Spirit at work in His church. We hope and pray for a better world, and then we act as if it will become a reality. Combine faith, hope, and love, and things get done. Change happens.

The real proof of the power of the gospel of Jesus Christ is its power to change lives.

As believers in Christ, we are in the life business—life today, life tomorrow, and life the next day. Yes, at the resurrection you will get a new body. Yes, one day there will be a new earth. But these vessels and this planet are not disposable or worthless. We aren't supposed to do just anything we want to them; we are God's assigned caretakers.

As imperfect as we humans are at the practice of faith, hope, and love, we have all experienced their ability to transform us. Our theology and, more importantly, our relationship with Jesus, drives us to care for our Father's planet and all His children.

The body of Christ was redeemed to be the hands and feet of God at work in the world, and where the hands and feet of God are at work, there is hope for creation and for all of humanity.

Reflections on Hope

One of my favorite children's books is The Little Engine That Could. *The story is about a big train that breaks down while carrying a load of toys and other good things to children who live on the other side of a mountain. The broken-down engine asks several other passing trains for help, but they are either unable or unwilling. Finally, he sees a tiny blue engine, and asks that (much smaller) engine if he'll pull the shipment of good things to the children on the other side of the mountain. The little train looks up at that huge mountain and the heavy shipment, and isn't sure he's up to the task. But finally he decides to give it a go. And all the way up the hill, our little hero puffs, "I think I can. I think I can. I think I can."*

Like that little train, we may feel like there's a huge mountain standing between us and the greener, cleaner world we long for. But Jesus had a few words for us about mountains. In Matthew 17:20, He says, "If you have faith as small as a mustard seed, you can say to this mountain, 'Move from here to there,' and it will move. Nothing will be impossible for you." With faith in God, nothing is impossible.

Living a green life is within the reach of every one of us. I think you can. God thinks you can. When the children from the next "valley"—from the next generation—see us and the world we pass on to them, my hope is that they'll see a generation that was green. My hope is that they'll see a generation that took its choices seriously, that placed its faith in God, and found the strength to climb the highest mountain. My hope is that they'll see a little generation that did.

—Emma Sleeth, daughter of Matthew and Nancy

Adapted with permission from *It's Easy Being Green* (Youth Specialties/Zondervan, 2007)

Session Notes: Hope

As you watch the final session film, **Hope**, use the following page to jot down notes, thoughts, and questions.

Hope Begins with a Changed Heart

1   *We see highways that get wider, more crowded, and more numerous. There are fewer and fewer flocks of birds in the sky. And if that doesn't get you down, just listen to predictions about the world's dwindling rainforests or freshwater supplies. All of this can be overwhelming—it can be depressing.*

—*Dr. Matthew Sleeth*

Hope isn't the first reaction most people have when considering the world's problems. Do the world's environmental problems seem overwhelming to you? How do you typically react when problems seem overwhelming? How does hope change your attitude?

2   Dr. Sleeth suggests that, as Christians, "We hope and pray for a better world, and then we act as if it will become a reality." Why are hope and faith so crucial to the environmental movement? What environmental changes do you hope and pray for? Do you act as if they will become a reality? Explain.

Dr. Sleeth states: "Combine faith, hope and love, and things get done. Change happens." Give an example of a situation that seemed hopeless, but when God and/or His people stepped in, change happened.

3

❝ *The power of the Bible doesn't lie in its ability to be proven scientifically, logically, or archaeologically. The real proof of the gospel is its power to change lives.* **❞**

—*Dr. Matthew Sleeth*

4

How could changing our lives to take better care of the environment serve as a witness for the gospel?

5 Dr. Sleeth suggests "the church brings unique contributions to creation care." What contributions can the church bring to resolving environmental problems?

6 Dr. Sleeth is often asked, "How do we move from worrying about problems to being part of the solution? How can we go from caring about God's creation to doing something to help?" How would you respond? How do we move from faith to action?

❝ *You will get a new body—and the earth will be renewed. But these vessels are not disposable or worthless. We aren't supposed to do just anything we want to them.* **❞**

7

—*Dr. Matthew Sleeth*

In what sense do we act as if our bodies are disposable? In what sense do we act as if the earth is disposable? Why must we be good stewards of both?

❝ *During our time on earth, we act as the body of Christ, as the hands and feet of life on the planet. If it means calling 911 when someone is having a heart attack, we should help. If it means feeding the hungry or clothing the naked, we do it. If it means cleaning up the water so the fish don't have mercury or dioxin, the body of Christ is called to action.* **❞**

8

—*Dr. Matthew Sleeth*

In what sense is caring for the planet intertwined with our call to feed the hungry and care for the poor? If we would call 911 to save *a* life, why aren't we (metaphorically) calling 911 to save *all* life?

9 What environmental legacy are you leaving for your grandchildren? What current actions can bring hope to future generations?

10

❝ *We shall awaken from our dullness and rise vigorously toward justice. If we fall in love with creation deeper and deeper, we will respond to its endangerment with passion.* ❞

—*Hildegard of Bingen (1098–1179)*

What factors have contributed to our "dullness" toward the environment? How can the church help us awaken and "rise vigorously toward justice"? How can "falling in love with creation deeper and deeper" help us "respond to its endangerment with passion"?

11

❝ *In a time of ecological emergency, the church can offer to the world a hope that is rooted in the power of God to bring new life into all that has been created.* ❞

—*Wesley Granberg-Michaelson (1945–), Ecology and Life*

How can you help "bring new life into all that has been created"?

A Changed Heart = A Changed Life

Christ the Gardener has returned! This is the good news: God's plan for redemption of the earth is no less bold or powerful than His original creative one. The difference is that although we were not part of His original creative team, we are invited onto the redemptive one.

In the gospel of Luke, a well-educated man asks Christ point-blank, "What must I do to inherit eternal life?" Jesus' answer sums up all of Scripture, and may be the most instructive passage regarding the world's environmental problems: "You shall love the Lord your God with all your heart, and with all your soul, and with all your strength, and with all your mind; and your neighbor as yourself" (Luke 10:27).

The questioner then asks, "Who is my neighbor?" In reply, Christ tells a story. A Jewish man is going down from Jerusalem to Jericho when he falls into the hands of robbers, who strip him, beat him, and leave him "half dead." Jesus then says a priest from the man's own religious group walks by the wounded man lying in the road, but offers no assistance. A second religious man comes along, a Levite. He sees the man, but instead of helping, crosses to the other side of the road and continues walking. Finally, a third man comes along, traveling on a donkey. He is a Samaritan, an ethnic and religious group despised by the Jews, and vice versa. But the Samaritan man is moved by compassion. He gets off his donkey and begins making bandages, using his own oil and wine to help the man. He then puts the wounded man on his donkey and pays for care at an inn, the equivalent of a hospital in that day. Lastly he agrees to pick up the bill for any additional care. Then Jesus asks his questioner: "Which of these three do you think was a neighbor to the man who fell into the hands of robbers?"

As an ER physician, I saw some 30,000 patients. Only once did someone come in and pay the hospital bill for a stranger.

This parable demonstrates a continuum of compassion, which can be applied to many problems, including the environment. The priest represents those of us who refuse to take any responsibility for environmental problems, even though we claim a close relationship with God. We close our eyes and walk on by. The second passerby, the Levite, is like most of us: he sees the problem, then says, "I should get back to Jerusalem and raise awareness. Maybe I'll blog on the problem of highway muggings, or send a letter off to the Roman centurion about beefing up patrols and installing better street lights." Like the Levite, we see the hardship caused by environmental problems, particularly for the poorest among us. Our hearts are moved to compassion, but we do little, if anything, to help because we don't want to be inconvenienced. Only the Samaritan, the one who is least likely to view the fallen Jewish man as his neighbor, takes action. He saw the need, and had mercy on him. Jesus tells us, as he told his questioner, "Go and do likewise."

What does this parable teach us about how we should approach environmental problems today? To have any lasting effect, our hearts must be moved by compassion for our fellow man and all of God's creation. We may find it dangerous. We may have to use our own resources. It may be inconvenient. It may be expensive. We may be ridiculed. We will have to take ongoing responsibility and make personal sacrifices. But such is the path to eternal life.

Everyone is our neighbor, including foreigners, strangers, people who hate us, and future generations. Perhaps the most important lesson of the Good Samaritan—the action that can separate us from the priest and Levite—is that we must "get off our donkey" before we can become part of the solution. The future will not be saved by our good intentions. It will be made better, or worse, only by our actions.

We show our love for the Lord by loving our neighbors. Every time we buy anything, or take any action, our family now asks two questions: Will this help me love God? And will this help me love my neighbor? The answer will always lead us to right action.

If we take shorter showers, carpool, or plant a tree, no one will necessarily notice or thank us. But if these things are done as an act to serve the Lord and to protect our neighbors, then we will have grown as loving, spiritual beings. Love is the great hope that the church offers the environmental movement.

—*Dr. Matthew Sleeth*

Adapted with permission from *The Green Bible* (HarperOne 2008)

Good Steward Action Plan: Hope

Instructions

In this final session, we will work on a comprehensive plan for action. Look over your previous goals, and select actions that will help you meet major goals in the months ahead.

For more ideas, visit the Resources page at blessedearth.org. In addition, *Go Green, Save Green* (www.gogreenthebook.com) has thousands of practical ideas that you can incorporate into your plan.

As the hands and feet of God, we have a responsibility to love what God loves and do what God does. My prayer is that, individually and together, we're faithful. In God's power and by His leading, hope starts here.

Today, Lord, help me to:

Select and accomplish at least four major goals (choose some of the examples below or write your own)

- Reduce my energy use by at least 10 percent.
- Cut back on trash production at home by 50 percent.
- Lead a Sunday school class using these films or the discussion guide in *Serve God, Save the Planet*.
- Start a green team at work, school, or church.
- Plan a community event or host a screening of the Blessed Earth films to raise awareness and inspire change.
- Organize an Earth Day Sunday event at church.
- Start a creation care column in my church bulletin.

1. _____

2. _____

3. _____

4. _____

Lord, help me *achieve these goals* through specific actions:

Goal 1: _____

Specific actions that will help me achieve this goal:

1. _____

2. _____

3. _____

4. _____

5. _____

Goal 2: _____

Specific actions that will help me achieve this goal:

1. _____

2. _____

3. _____

4. _____

5. _____

Goal 3:

Specific actions that will help me achieve this goal:

1.

2.

3.

4.

5.

Goal 4: _____

Specific actions that will help me achieve this goal:

1. _____

2. _____

3. _____

4. _____

5. _____

❝ _Heavenly Father, thank You for the hope that You gave us through Your Son, Jesus. Conform me to the resurrected image of Christ, the Gardener, and fill me with hope for a greener, more sustainable planet. As You increase my desire to tend and care for Your garden, teach me to stay scripturally grounded. Help me to press forward with resolve, tenderness, and a loving heart. Amen._ ❞

Digging Deeper: *What Scripture Says About Hope*

Scripture calls us to put our hope in God rather than in the things of this world. "Command those who are rich in this present world not to be arrogant nor to put their hope in wealth, which is so uncertain, but to put their hope in God, who richly provides us with everything." *(1 Timothy 6:16-18)*

Hope is having faith in things *not seen* rather than in things seen. "Now faith is being sure of what we hope for and certain of what we do not see." *(Hebrews 11:1–3)* "But hope that is seen is no hope at all. Who hopes for what he already has?" *(Romans 8:23–25)*

Hope in God gives us boldness, confidence, and strength. "Therefore, since we have such a hope, we are very bold." *(2 Corinthians 3:11–13)* "For you have been my hope, O Sovereign LORD, my confidence since my youth." *(Psalm 71:4–6)* "Be strong and take heart, all you who hope in the LORD." *(Psalm 31:23–24)*

Our hope is eternal. "But as for me, I will always have hope; I will praise you more and more." *(Psalm 71:14)* "There is surely a future hope for you, and your hope will not be cut off." *(Proverbs 23:17–19)*

Hope changes our perspective on problems and hardship. "Brothers, we do not want you to be ignorant about those who fall asleep, or to grieve like the rest of men, who have no hope." *(1 Thessalonians 4:12–14)* "Why are you downcast, O my soul? Why so disturbed within me? Put your hope in God, for I will yet praise him, my Savior and my God." *(Psalm 42:10–11)*

Our hope is in God's love, and this hope does not disappoint. "O Israel, put your hope in the LORD, for with the LORD is unfailing love and with him is full redemption." *(Psalm 130:6–8)* "And hope does not disappoint us, because God has poured out his love into our hearts by the Holy Spirit, whom he has given us." *(Romans 5:4–6)*

God wants us to seek encouragement in His promises. "You are my refuge and my shield; I have put my hope in your word." *(Psalm 119:113–115).* "I rise before dawn and cry for help; I have put my hope in your word." *(Psalm 119:146–148)*

As the hands and feet of God on earth, we are to act in hope. "There-fore, prepare your minds for action; be self-controlled; set your hope fully on the grace to be given you when Jesus Christ is revealed." *(1 Peter 1:12–14)* "[L]et us be self-controlled, putting on faith and love as a breast-plate, and the hope of salvation as a helmet." *(1 Thessalonians 5:7–9)*

God is faithful to those who place their hope in Him. "You answer us with awesome deeds of righteousness, O God our Savior, the hope of all the ends of the earth and of the farthest seas." *(Psalm 65:4–6)* "But Christ is faithful as a son over God's house. And we are his house, if we hold on to our courage and the hope of which we boast." *(Hebrews 3:5–7)*

Hope inspires endurance. "We continually remember before our God and Father your work produced by faith, your labor prompted by love, and your endurance inspired by hope in our Lord Jesus Christ." *(1 Thessalonians 1:2-4)*

Adapted with permission from *The Gospel According to the Earth: Why the Good Book Is a Green Book* by Matthew Sleeth (HarperOne, 2010)

❝ *The Bible makes it clear that our hope isn't just hope in heaven or faith that better days are coming someday in eternity, but faith in the real presence and power of the Holy Spirit at work in and through us today to do what, without Him, would be impossible. It is only through God's power that we have the strength or ability to do God's will, whether it's making disciples or working to protect and share the resources He's given us. In God's power, we have hope that it is possible to tend and protect the garden He's placed us in.* **❞**

—*Dr. Matthew Sleeth*

Acknowledgments

This book couldn't have happened without the creative genius of Santino Stoner and David Wenzel. God led us to break bread with you nearly three years ago along the river near Grand Rapids; thank you for your strength and perseverance as we paddled upstream together.

Brett and Corey—we are grateful for your immense talents and your friendship. To the entire Dot&Cross dream team—including Sue, Seth, Michael, and Sally—your belief in our work keeps us going.

We also thank God for our partners at Zondervan—especially John Raymond, Michael Cook, and Sandra Vander Zicht—we are grateful for your willingness to walk with us in faith.

To our partners at HarperOne—including Mickey Maudlin, Emily Grandstaff, and Marlene Baer—thanks for believing in the creation care message and helping us share it with the world.

To our friends and neighbors at Asbury Seminary—including Tom Tumblin, Ginny Proctor, Leslie Andrews, Ellsworth Kallas, and Tim Tennent—it is an honor to reach out to God's kingdom along side of you.

To Will Sears: you are an answer to prayer. Blessed Earth is indeed blessed by your many talents.

Finally, our loving thanks to the Kendeda Foundation: your generosity, encouragement, and faithful support of Blessed Earth have helped us move mountains.

About Blessed Earth

Blessed Earth is an educational nonprofit that inspires and equips faith communities to become better stewards of the earth. Through outreach to churches, campuses, and media we build bridges that promote measurable environmental change and meaningful spiritual growth.

The Sleeth family's environmental journey has paralleled their faith journey. As they began to live out what it means to love God with all their heart, mind, soul, and strength, and to love their neighbors as themselves, they found their calling: to live more simply. The first and most important miracle for the Sleeths is that their entire family came to know Christ, not just in their heads but in their daily actions. Hanging clothes on the line, washing dishes by hand, and growing their own food are all ways of how they show daily respect for God's creation, and love for their global neighbors.

From these humble beginnings a revolutionary ministry began to grow. Dr. Sleeth wrote a book that received a much wider, more enthusiastic response than he could have ever dreamed. Then, to address larger audiences and respond to the hundreds of speaking requests, the Sleeths formed Blessed Earth. The Sleeths' message has inspired congregations, colleges, and individuals that never had creation care on their radar screen to make huge changes, quickly. When people embrace the principles of simplicity and conservation in their hearts, the difference is dramatic.

Focusing less on material things, and more on relationships with family, friends, and God, leads to happier, more meaningful, and richer lives. With God, all things are possible—including a cleaner, healthier world to leave for future generations.

Additional Resources

Also available from the Sleeths and Blessed Earth:

Blessed Earth: Part 1—Hope for Creation
Zondervan, 2010.

In *Hope for Creation*, Dr. Sleeth explores his personal salvation experience and desire to follow Jesus in the context of the love story God tells "in the beginning." In these first six sessions, Dr. Sleeth guides the viewer through each of the created elements—Light, Water, Soil, Heavens, Animals, and Man—and redefines what it means to save the planet.

Blessed Earth: Part 1—Hope for Creation Guidebook
Zondervan, 2010.

Designed for use with the *Hope for Creation* DVD, this guidebook provides personal questions, practical applications, and additional content to help viewers dig deeper into the creation care lessons of Sessions 1–6. An accompanying Leader's Guide for group discussion is available at blessedearth.org.

Serve God, Save the Planet
Zondervan, 2007.

Dr. Matthew Sleeth and his family lived in a big house on the coast, had two luxury cars, and many material possessions. As chief of the medical staff at a large hospital, Sleeth was living the American dream—until he saw an increasing number of his patients suffering from cancer, asthma, and other chronic diseases. Suspecting that the earth and its inhabitants were in trouble, he turned to Jesus for guidance. Dr. Sleeth shares how his family cut their use of resources by more than two-thirds and discovered how the scriptural lessons of personal responsibility, simplicity, and stewardship could lead to a healthier, more joyful life.

Go Green, Save Green
Tyndale House Publishers, 2009.

Many people want to "go green" but put it off because they believe it's too time consuming and too expensive. Not so! Nancy Sleeth and her family have been living an eco-friendly lifestyle for years, saving both time and money. Now, for the first time, she divulges hundreds of practical, easy-to-implement steps that you can take to create substantial money savings while protecting the earth.

It's Easy Being Green
Zondervan/Youth Specialties, 2008.

Want to set your teens on fire for Christ and all of creation? Just fifteen years old when she wrote *It's Easy Being Green*, author/activist Emma Sleeth is a rebel with a cause: saving souls while saving the planet. With real stories from real life, Emma explores how everything we do—from what we eat to how we spend our spare time—impacts the world.

The Gospel According to the Earth
HarperOne, 2010.

In *The Gospel According to the Earth*, Matthew Sleeth retells the often radically countercultural Bible stories that motivated his journey from emergency room doctor to environmental leader, and shows Christians what they can do to care for God's green earth. With passion and faith, Sleeth provides a new green lens through which we can read the Bible to discover answers to our biggest questions of our time and helps us to see afresh how relevant, broad, and deep the Bible's teaching remains.

For more information about the Creation Care journey, visit blessedearth.org,
where you'll find the most comprehensive, interactive Creation Care resources on the web.